PC
JOU

Volume X

THE POWYS SOCIETY

The Powys Society is a registered charity, No. 801332

The Powys Society was founded in 1967 to 'establish the true literary status of the Powys family through promotion of the reading and discussion of their works', in particular those of John Cowper Powys (1872–1963), Theodore Francis Powys (1875–1953), and Llewelyn Powys (1884–1939).

The Society publishes a journal and three newsletters a year, and has embarked on a publication programme. In addition it organises an annual weekend conference, occasional meetings, exhibitions, and walks in areas associated with the Powys family.

The Society is an international one, attracting scholars and non-academics from around the world, and welcomes everyone interested in learning more about this remarkable family.

Correspondence and membership enquiries should be addressed to:

Chris Gostick, Hon. Secretary
The Old School House, George Green Road, George Green, Wexham, Buckinghamshire, SL3 6BJ
(tel: 01753 578632; e-mail: gostick@altavista.net)

Visit the Powys Society Web Site:
http://www.iaehv.nl/users/tklijn/pws/powys.htm

THE POWYS JOURNAL

Volume X

2000

Editor
Paul Roberts

Contributing Editor
Charles Lock

THE POWYS SOCIETY

The Powys Journal is a publication of The Powys Society, appearing annually each summer. Its aim is to publish original material by the Powys family — in particular, John Cowper Powys, Theodore Francis Powys and Llewelyn Powys — and scholarly articles and other material relating to them and their circle. It also carries reviews of books by and about the Powys family and their circle.

The Powys Journal is grateful to the copyright holders of the individual estates and their literary agents for their permission to quote from the writings of John Cowper Powys, Theodore Francis Powys, A. R. Powys, Llewelyn Powys, and Philippa Powys.

MSS for publication, correspondence about the contents of the *Journal*, and books for review should be addressed to the Hon. Secretary. *The Powys Journal* has a refereeing policy, whereby material is submitted for independent reports, in which the anonymity of the author and the referee is preserved. MSS should, therefore, be submitted in duplicate, or on disk in ASCII or text-only format (as well as in your own wordprocessor) with one paper copy, with the name and address of the author on a separate sheet. MSS will be acknowledged but cannot be returned unless accompanied by a stamped, self-addressed envelope. Authors of printed articles will receive two copies of the *Journal*.

Orders for copies of the *Journal* should be addressed to the Society's Publications Manager, Stephen Powys Marks, Hamilton's, Kilmersdon, near Bath, Somerset, BA3 5TE (tel. 01761 435134).

The photographs on pages 6, 147 and 180 are reproduced by cour tesy of Stephen Powys Marks.

Cover and title-page design: Bev Craven

Typeset in Garamond
in PageMaker 6.5 on a Macintosh computer
by Stephen Powys Marks

Printed by Anthony Williams, printer (tel: 0117 986 0431)

ISSN 0962–7057

ISBN 1 874559 23 6

CONTENTS

Powys family group on the steps of the stables at Montacute Vicarage, 1910.
front row: Isobel Powys, Mary Cowper Powys, Charles Francis Powys
middle row: Maria Theodora Johnson ('Aunt Dora'), Katie Powys
behind left: Gertrude Powys   top: Dorothy Mary Powys

Editorial

It is a great honour to have been invited to edit this special, tenth anniversary issue of *The Powys Journal*, although more than a little daunting to have to follow the outstanding work done by Louise de Bruin, Peter J. Foss and John R. Williams in establishing its fine reputation as a leading repository of Powys scholarship.

Having accepted the invitation, I knew at once what kind of *Journal* I wanted to produce: an issue devoted almost entirely to previously unpublished works by members of the Powys family. Research amongst our members has shown that this is the sort of material they most want to read, and there could surely be no more fitting way of celebrating this important milestone in the Society's progress.

In the case of T. F. Powys, contractual arrangements made it impossible to publish any of his unpublished fiction. However, we are in the fortunate position of having a number of short, unpublished manuscript essays in the Society's collection and these, together with the fascinating and learned commentaries by J. Lawrence Mitchell and John R. Williams, provide a valuable insight into the development of Theodore Powys's style. Although they are relatively brief, any manuscripts which can elicit responses citing Nietzsche, Whitman, Blake, Wordsworth and *The Rubaiyat of Omar Khayyam*, and which demonstrate so clearly the path of their author's progress, must surely be worthy of publication.

The unpublished material by Llewelyn Powys which Peter J. Foss has edited for this issue of the *Journal* also does much to reveal its author's working methods. 'An Exile's Return' is not only intrinsically interesting but also, as Foss points out, gives us cause to reconsider the way in which some of Llewelyn Powys's posthumously published material has been used, as well as alerting readers to the way in which Powys himself reshaped autobiographical material for literary purposes. It is a mark of the genius of Llewelyn Powys that his powerful evocations of sensual experience can so easily lure us into the assumption that what we are reading is a simple and direct transcription of actual events, rather than a work of literary creation. In alerting us to the dangers of such easy assumptions, Peter J. Foss emphasises once again just how wonderful a writer Llewelyn Powys is and why he is so often the member of the family to first attract new readers.

That he was able to command both admiration and devotion amongst those who came to know him personally is demonstrated in Llewelyn Powys's letters to H. G. Tavender, which provide us with an invaluable insight into his working methods.

The unpublished works of John Cowper Powys offer perhaps the most fruitful source of interesting new material, simply because they are so much more abundant. Nevertheless, in selecting work for publication in this issue of the *Journal* I have attempted to do two things above all else: to provide material from a comparatively ill-explored epoch in the author's life and to bring together works which are both thematically consistent and mutually illuminating. The early play 'The Entermores' not only gives us a portrait (one-sided though it must inevitably be) of John Cowper's life with his wife Margaret, but also embodies with unexpected impartiality the philosophy which he was then developing through essays such as 'The New Paganism'. I am very grateful to Glen Cavaliero for his commentary on 'The Entermores' which, in his inimitable way, places the work firmly in its personal, social and literary context.

Albert Reginald Powys is widely known and respected as an architect and architectural historian. It is, therefore, all the more interesting to find him venturing into the very different realm of social policy in the essay published for the first time here. Again, I am deeply grateful to Stephen Powys Marks, the author's grandson, for preparing the piece for publication and for his illuminating comments.

The relationship between Stephen Reynolds and Katie Powys is one of those things with which all Powysians will be vaguely familiar. Now, however, thanks to the remarkable work of Christopher Scoble, Stephen Reynolds can at last become more than just a name and the details of the relationship which, quite innocently, pushed the ever-sensitive Katie over the threshold of madness can be clearly understood. We are fortunate indeed in having secured permission to include pre-publication extracts from Christopher Scoble's forthcoming book *Fisherman's Friend: A life of Stephen Reynolds* (which is to be published by Halsgrove in November of this year) in this issue of the *Journal*. Not only is it of enormous interest in itself, but it also brings to light lengthy passages from the diaries of Katie Powys, which have previously been discussed by Angela Pitt in *The Powys Journal* Volume II (1992) and from which extracts have been published in Volume V (1995). Also included in Christopher Scoble's book are long passages from Katie Powys's prose-poem 'Phoenix', which I suspect most of us had mistakenly assumed was not much longer than the page or so published in *The Dial* in 1928. Is it too much to hope that, as a result of Christopher's work, the possibility of publishing 'Phoenix' in its entirety might be explored?

I hope that members of the Society will feel that the material collected in this issue of the *Journal* is worthy of the occasion and that it might also be seen as a fitting memorial to Isobel Powys Marks, Oliver Wilkinson, Martin Rivers Pollock, and Derek Langridge, friends and mentors we have lost in the past year.

ACKNOWLEDGMENTS

In addition to the named contributors, I am grateful to the following for the support they have given to the publication of this issue of the *Journal*: Gerard Casey, Sally Connely, Louise de Bruin, Shelagh Powys Hancox, Morine Krissdóttir, Gerald Pollinger, John Powys, and Cecil Woolf.

THEODORE FRANCIS POWYS

Three Meditations

On Friendship

I do not know what this word Friendship means. Has it perchance some strange mystical interpretation, some sign that proclaims a hidden goodness in man? Many wise men have spoken much concerning it, for it draws all men to it, as a loadstone in the darkness, and when found it is colder than stone and harder than brass.

Francis Bacon holds that friendship opens man's heart as an aperient would open his bowels. He believes that man's life is not compleat without friendship, that man should bestow it upon someone or, being kept within him, like an ill humour it will gather corruption. Francis Bacon errs in his conception of Friendship, and after him all writers have been found wanting, for knowledge in this matter has been hid from them.

The sages who uttered sacred words, words named sacred because of their God-like wisdom, have never spoken confusion on this matter.

In their old wisdom I find but small allusion to the friend, nor comes it in any religion. Where has the friend a worshipper, a temple, or friendship a poet to praise her?

To my mind the love of David for Jonathan was a matter far different from friendship.

Did Christ or Zoroaster call their disciples friends?

Does Solomon say 'my friends'? No, but rather, 'my son'.

How lovingly we say 'my father', 'my son', 'my brother', 'my home'. With what little relish do we say 'our friends'.

Among our Moderns only one, a wild and rough spirit, has seen full well the lie of friendship. Yet this one, who saw nobleness in all, has clasped friendship to his breast, and has cried with a loud voice not 'friendship', but 'comradeship' is eternal. He has said, 'O my companions, Ye that grow with me in this plot or little garden, I grow near to you all. I am your companion'. Behold this strange wild voice has spoken truth; the little plants know it, the trees of the field know, and the live animals understand.

There are plants that the gardener knows will not grow together, there are animals that do battle if near one another, and there are men that can never agree. But the companion is one that grows well with you.

By the old ancestor worship has God spoken, by the worship of the great tree, by Solomon and the old sages, by Christ has he spoken, and by many prophets.

He has said that the ties of kinship are stronger than iron, and has brought all men from Adam. He would have all men brothers: brothers, not friends.

Man hath ever tried to escape the eternal laws of the universe. He has tried to bend the colossal wisdom of the destinies, to turn them aside, so that his own way may be sweet and his own path easy to traverse. To him the smooth way seemed ever the best, and the way of lies easy for his feet. Man finds the twisted way of shame easier than the strong hills of truth, for in high places truth lives and in a strong clear air.

Man believes in charity and friendship, but in cold and hunger he dares not believe. That which rots and becomes corruption he loves, that which abides always and is strong does he hate.

And one asked, 'How shall this be?' and 'What means this?' and 'What is companionship?'

'It has no meaning save in the laws of Eternity, there it is graven as the stars, in depth as the sea of darkness, and wonderful as the eternal light; a law as fixed as gravitation, that alters not, until the essence of things come.

O for one to make man acknowledge the strong laws, that alter not, that are eternal.

Could men see them, they would leave clinging to false words, friendship and the like. They would know the laws that are so terrible to them. They would see their wisdom and by their means, as by the strong hands of help, they would stretch themselves, as giants with a new strength. They would leave false weakness behind, and climb the steep hills, with the new light of youth. There are no friends. There are brothers.

On God

Beyond and before God cometh Fear and when Fear findeth an entrance into the heart of man, this word God cometh in also.

The cultured and merry Greeks, having employed many stratagems against Fear, at length decided to destroy this His companion, and so thought to get Him out of their company. Toward the end they paid their priests so well and looked so little into their morals that they soon found they came into no man's company, only frequenting the tavern and brothel, leaving the worthy people, their neighbours, to live as they desired.

A nobler nation there is, of a greater and more wonderful glory than the Greeks, whose history, so terrible and sad, has cast a heavy shadow over the whole world. This nation are called Jews.

It was said of them once that they desired a king. Now I read this word to mean not king, but God, for all nations began with kings and the idea that the people would desire a king seemeth to me impossible. These Jews were ruled at first by their wise men, who made just laws; yet the people became weak and the yoke of Moses seemed hard for them, so they must needs cry out for a God.

The god of Abraham, Isaac, and Jacob must indeed be great and yet the prayer, 'O Abraham, O Isaac, O Jacob,' hath a deeper sound than 'Almighty Jehovah'.

Here in this island, with us who live in this age of iron, it seems that God rests, a commercial figure set in a cage of gold and hid in the midst of a cloud, His mind a strange medley of wrath, covetousness and doting fondness, His love the love of a young and foolish girl. The weakness of man hath desired this God, and has found him. Man has graven Him out of his own mind's folly. Better are the obscure and vulgar that worship wood and stone, for wood and stone have their hardness and strength, but this God is weak as a shadow. Surely we would have the truth of men and gods, surely we would hold this god, and see whether He be God or no. The rock of ages we break, and we find a shadow of nothingness.

And yet we cling round the remembrance of this one word more than all our sorrows and joys. It is our loadstone, our wonder, our desire, our Father, a sound of childhood, of trust, of comfort, a strong one, the mighty, He who cleaves the night air. Yet verily do we dishonour this strange one when we make Him a slave to our weakness, a pander to our lusts, a collector of our debts. We hold Him up as an axe to strike our enemies, a torment for our friends, and a punishment for our children. We change His name from God to Devil and from Devil to God. We defile Him with our false words, we spit at Him with soft prayers, we curse Him with sweet music. We will in no wise let Him alone, but must always howl out His name, with curses and imprecations, with cries and tears. We pray to God, calling Him wise, merciful, all-powerful, we magnify His name, and would indeed place Him amongst the princes. He is our saviour, our friend, our father, our all, yet our smallest possession we account of more worth than He. Our minds are inclined ever toward the earth, yet we must needs pretend to love heaven.

We are ruled by the great law of hunger and after that to procreate our kind; these are our real gods, our kings, our governors, they rule our whole hour of labour. But when we have food and wines, our play time comes and we fill our lands with lazy drones, priests, temples, prayers, poems etc. as toys, dolls, puppets and dancing dogs. Then we buy racks, curses, the stake. All this we do to worship God.

I asked once a wise man to explain and make clear this matter and he sent unto me out of his hut a little old woman with a great beard and scarce two teeth in her head, who spake thus unto me with signs.

She dug a hole in the earth, and burying her head therein she seemed to listen for a good while, then she shook off the mould from her hair, and kissed the earth. And I knew that she desired to hide her thoughts in the earth where they might grow and I heard a voice that said 'Man is the soil, and not the plant, and the racecourse and not the runner. And he that finds his God must lose him.'

On A Future Life

This letter I write unto Mr Feeblemind and unto all his kindred upon the Earth.

Man desires to live, yet his reason tells him he must die.

Solomon infers that, to the downtrodden, death is good, but to the rich it is bad; yet all men do not live in the extreme, a middle sort remains of whom Solomon speaks not, save that he sends all men to nature to consider the justness of God. This is good, but does not satisfy all minds, for this desire of man to live is not put off by reason. Man does not say, 'I see all things end, therefore do I likewise desire my own end.'

Man desires to live; from the beginning he willed life, and to the end he shall live it.

Philosophy to the wise and strong is a good food, but it causes the weak to fear. Modern philosophy is but the old word of Solomon again remembered. It sends man to nature to learn that nothing dies, and that man himself returns again, and will again return until the end of Time.

Man is part of earth and has lived since its beginning and will live until its end. Thus does philosophy help the strong, but it leaves the weak in an ill-taking. Now let us learn how to console the weak and save poor feeble minds from despair.

We are now thirty years of age and look back towards childhood as to a long distant dream. We remember the ways of our sister, the manner of our brother equally well, indeed we might have been them. And we ourselves might as well have been other men living in times past, for we see in their writings tales of ourselves, our ways, our actions. It is no more miraculous to have lived before in this world, than to have lived here as children, seeing we remember so little of either period. We are children of life as well as of sleep and of death, and must pass through these three changes.

But I see poor Feeblemind is not contented, neither does he understand me very well. He falls ever over that same cliff of death and corruption, and sees the charnel house, the shroud and the coffin. He says 'Where man falls, there shall he lie', and he sees in the grave a pit of black darkness. He says 'How can man enter again into the womb and live?'

But I answer, 'This is a small matter, for when life itself is explained all these things shall be understood'. I think we may well trust to the economy in nature, for she that has a use for all things would never create new life when the old could be used. She will not allow the fool to remain in his folly, but brings him again to the earth so that he may get wisdom. And what is time in the eyes of the truth, for man must learn wisdom and shall return again and ever again until his eyes be opened.

As to the time that man remains dead, and how he enters the womb again, we understand no more than life itself, but we see that the babe sleeps a deep sleep in the womb of his mother for nine months, and perchance a man may sleep nine years in the earth, ere ever he returns to life again: but this is mere conjecture. That which is a law and a truth in one department of Nature is impossible to become a lie and a fraud in another.

In all ways nature is the same and alters not, for she is God. The sea is carried to the clouds and returns to the rivers, and again runs down unto the sea. And if God can cause matter to come again to the same place, can he not do the same to life also? Was it a horrible thing to sleep in the womb for nine months, and will it be horrible to sleep a little while in the earth's womb? Exactly the time of rest that we need, that rest shall we have and no more.

Fear not, poor Feeblemind. Did not Christ say 'Man shall be born again'?

NOTE ON THE TEXT

The text of 'Three Meditations' is constructed from three separate manuscripts which are part of the Bissell Gift to The Powys Society and are held at the Dorset County Museum.

Two of the pieces ('On God' and 'On Friendship') appear together in an Acme exercise book, which bears the name of Violet R. Dodds, in her own hand, on the top right-hand corner of the front cover.

'On A Future Life' is a separate manuscript and the reference to T. F. Powys being 'now thirty years of age' allows us to date this particular piece to 1905. Similarities in style and content suggest that the other pieces belong to the same period.

It was in 1904 that Theodore Powys moved to East Chaldon in Dorset, where he soon met Violet Dodds, a village girl of eighteen. He proposed to her in February 1905 and they were married within three months. Since there is no reason to believe that Violet herself had any need of an Acme exercise book, it seems likely that 'On Friendship' and 'On God' belong to, or slightly before, the period of her engagement to Theodore, that is 1904–05.

P. R.

THEODORE FRANCIS POWYS

Cheriton

It is curious how the mere fact of living in the country quiet brings us, if our souls are receptive, very near to the sublime.

The art of the country is the art of the humble sod. The simple people who live in Cheriton move and have their being where the very voice of the earth speaks in a language that they know. They are the thing in itself, they feel instinctively what so many try all their lives to feel and only now and again do catch a glimpse of.

Not a leaf moves, not a breath of wind passes over the land, but it gives a new word to the dwellers in Cheriton. We live deep, we wrap ourselves secure in the folds of the living earth. We move, we of Cheriton, in an atmosphere that is almost unknown in the town. Slowly and surely our lives become the same yesterday, today and forever. We take and eat our bread, we move from the rick yards to the field, from the field to the barn. We cross the narrow bridge that leads to our cottage, holding our lantern in our hand — a moving star at nightfall — and our minds are sustained by the coming of the night and the coming of the morn. All things become one to us, whether we wake, whether we sleep, whether we plough, whether we sow, whether we go to the field or whether we return from the field. For our steps have the same tread whatsoever we do.

It is curious how the feeling of the artist and the feeling of him who lives in the bosom of the earth meet and merge and become at certain times almost the same feeling.

This I have learned of Cheriton, to feed upon the true art of the earth-life with faith in believing. I have only to see the form of a man standing lonely in a field in order to be filled with the sense of the mystery, with the sense of the wonder of life. The shaking of a tree in the wind tells me now that the Father of all breathes upon it. I have but to see a child pass my gate and all the world of romance that is hidden in one little life fills my mind. I see an old woman go by and I see not only her but all the woe, all the sorrows, all the joys that go to make up a human life. I see her as a child again — she is running gaily in the sweet season of spring, she holds may buds in her hands. I see her in her last long sleep.

Oh, divine art of life, that can change the refuse of time into the spring flowers, the most woeful body of flesh and blood can be changed by thee. Take us and change us, give to us the eyes that can see wonder in all. Give to us the sense that can see deep into the mystery, so that no human thing can be for us a thing forsaken, and no sad sight come without finding out our tears.

I hear a human voice. Because it is a common thing to hear, is it therefore the less wonderful to hear it?

I hear a human step out on the road. 'Tis but my neighbour perchance, but 'tis also something more than my neighbour. Oh, power of affection! Oh, seeing eye of Christ that can in a moment turn stones into bread and give to the most humble step of a mortal an eternal sound. If only all men knew our secret, if only all men felt themselves as we in simple Cheriton feel ourselves, though often we know it not, to be the flesh and blood of a real, living world, what a different thing life would be from what it is now.

All things can be wrought by the mind. We can mould our surroundings as we choose. We can, by the power of affection, give an immortal being to any human form. The world is as we wish it to be. We can view a village such as this humble Cheriton as a mere stagnation, as simply a gossip-ground of foolish talk, or else we can see it all as immortal writings written upon the sod; a marvel of words, in which blood is used as the ink and human lives are the letters. But who can tell the meaning of the writing?

The shepherd is now slowly climbing up the hill behind his flock, the dairy maid is gaily calling to the cows, a dog barks at the farm. 'Tis a picture as old as man. Human matters, human matters. Let us love it as we should love all human pictures if we were wise.

There is, I know, so much in Cheriton that seems to be but the clatter of tongues in a smoky tavern. But the picture is old and true and well mellowed in the sweet pastoral airs. Oh, Cheriton, with your heathy places, with your wind-swept hills and fair lowland meadows, with your human hearts and your human voices, let me never turn from you, for I love you.

Let the world go dance on, I have my task.

Let all the runners run by and I, I still stoop over the sod, for the human picture that God hath coloured, no man can change.

NOTE ON THE TEXT

The nine-page manuscript of 'Cheriton' is part of the Bissell Gift to The Powys Society and is housed at the Dorset County Museum.

At the top of the first page Powys has written 'The typed copy of this has gone to America in the hope of its being taken in some paper or other.' This comment, although not conclusive, may help us to date the manuscript, for Louis Wilkinson tells us in *Welsh Ambassadors* that 'In November 1905, he [T. F. P] wrote me a letter beginning with a reference to some stories of his which John had taken to America earlier in that year. I was in America that November, but John was not, so the stories were handed back to me.' [Chapman and Hall, 1936, 71]

There are several Cheritons listed in the gazetteer, but none appear to have any connection with T. F. Powys. The name seems a simple device by which Powys could extol the beauties of Chaldon whilst disguising its true identity from any who might be tempted to explore its lanes for themselves.

P. R.

COMMENTARY I

The best known image of Walt Whitman shows him already aged at sixty-eight, but bearded and benevolent, in the luminous 1887 painting by Thomas Eakins. For most people, 'the Good Gray Poet' is the only Whitman, one worthy of enshrinement as unofficial poet laureate. This image quite obliterates that of the egotistical and subversive freethinker who shocked his contemporaries and was dubbed 'disgraceful' by the reclusive Emily Dickinson. Of course, to earn acceptance by the public, Whitman had to domesticate himself, to reshape both his image and his work: *Leaves of Grass* was a work-in-progress, a poetic self-fashioning from its initial appearance in 1855 through nine editions until the poet's death in 1892.

At about the same age (sixty-seven), the Theodore Powys of Douglas Glass's photograph appears somewhat remote, the stern patriarch, if not quite the hermit, of East Chaldon. In this photograph, it is easier to attribute 'insatiable carefulness' to him than 'unappeasable imagination', though Sylvia Townsend Warner credited him with both characteristics ('Two Extracts from a Study of Theodore Powys', *A Chatto & Windus Miscellany*, 1928, 55). We know him best as the author of *Mr. Weston's Good Wine*, *Fables*, and the kind of short stories so judiciously selected by Charles Prentice in *God's Eyes A-Twinkle*. However, as we move back in compositional time, the Powysian path/work becomes increasingly unfamiliar. Those who love *Mr. Weston* cannot necessarily abide *Mr. Tasker*; and, for many readers, *The Soliloquy of a Hermit* (1916) must remain more of an interesting document — a spiritual autobiography perhaps, or a portrait of the artist a-borning — rather than an accomplished work of art. By the time we find ourselves before *An Interpretation of Genesis* (1907), the very earliest of Theodore's 'published' works, we are in very different territory indeed. *An Interpretation* was his first attempt — in dialogue form — at commentary on all the books of the Old Testament. He cast himself in the role of Zetetes (the Seeker) and the exchanges with the Lawgiver of Israel are in the elevated, but intimate, language of 'thou' and 'I'. This is at once the style of Fitzgerald's *Rubaiyat of Omar Khayyam* (1859) and of Nietzsche's

Thus Spake Zarathustra (translated by Alexander Tille in 1886). It is not therefore irrelevant that, in his copy of Nietzsche's work, Theodore inscribed stanza 73 of the *Rubaiyat*:

> Ah Love! Could thou and I with fate conspire
> To grasp this sorry scheme of things entire
> Would we not shatter it to bits — and then
> Re-mould it nearer to the Heart's Desire.

What is striking about almost all the early works of Theodore Powys is that they are first-person narratives; whereas the published author we know wrote almost exclusively in the third person, with rare exceptions such as 'The House with an Echo'. We might argue, with some validity, that these early first-person narratives appear to reflect the naïve egocentrism of a young man who can see the world only from his own perspective. But Theodore's youthful faith in himself had been severely shaken by his farming experiences and his reading had been his salvation. No doubt that is why he proved so responsive to Nietzsche's message of self-love and self-assertion, especially: 'The Thou is older than the I; the Thou hath been consecrated but not yet the I' (XVI, *Neighbour-Love*). In an early version of 'This is Thyself' there occurs a revealing passage, later suppressed, which records the occasion of his 'discovery' of Nietzsche, some time between Christmas Day 1898 (the date he copied out the passage from *Omar Khayyam*) and Nietzsche's death in 1900:

> One day I left the fields, and entered a wood. There was a pile of faggots, old sticks left from the winter. I sat upon them and read *Thus Spake Zarathustra* ... It was not nature that I had to get attuned to, it was man ... I felt all this as I lay in the woods on those winter faggots and this German fellow compelled me to look at men and cows ... This book spoke to me, the author was not dead then but near death, and he spoke to me.

Here then is the fount and the source: Nietzsche pointed the way and Whitman provided the example with 'I celebrate myself, and sing myself.' Nonetheless, from a purely narrative perspective, there were risks attached to Theodore's reliance upon first-person narrative, particularly in fiction. Mrs Stracey, his loyal correspondent and critic from his earliest days in Chaldon, identified the problem in her frank response to 'Under the Bondage of Fear' (HRHRC, January–March, 1904), Theodore's first turgid efforts at a novel: 'All this introductory bit wants rewriting with more simplicity and clearness.' More pointedly, she admonished him: 'Now I think it would be much better if you gave this all as Jake's own thoughts — in a work of this kind the reader does not want to know what the author thinks; he is concerned with the hero — and him only.' Unfortunately, his quest for an appropriate narrative voice would prove to be an extended one. As Louis Wilkinson accurately observed in *Welsh Ambassadors* (1936): 'Theodore's power in writing matured so slowly that his doubts of it were natural ones' (65). In fact, the critical breakthrough did not occur until *The Soliloquy of a Hermit*, the first part of which is in the first person, whereas the second part witnesses a split between the narrator and the 'I' who becomes Mr Thomas (67).

Even if we lacked internal and external clues sufficient to date 'Cheriton' and 'Three Meditations' precisely, the language of these pieces would betray them as early work. All, for example, are unsophisticated first-person narratives of the sort characteristic of Theodore's securely dated early work. And all offer substantial internal clues of style and content that suggest the influences that shaped them. In the essay 'On Friendship', 'the wild and rough spirit' who calls men 'comrades' and 'brothers' is surely Walt Whitman. It was Whitman who described himself as 'one of the roughs' in an anonymous 1855 review of his own work; and in 'Song of Myself' he claims 'that all the men ever born are also my brothers'. Theodore, of course, owned a volume of selections from *Leaves of Grass* — in essence an expurgated edition, almost certainly that first prepared by William Michael Rossetti with the author's help (see *Poems*, Bissell Collection) and he would have read Havelock Ellis's chapter on Whitman in *The New Spirit* (Bissell Collection; Theodore's copy is dated September 7, 1900). Whitman's work was a topic of discussion among family and friends too. Brother John had lectured on Whitman in Liverpool in February 1906; and, when Theodore asserted in his commentary on Ezekiel that 'the virgin must be defiled before she can become a Mother', Mrs Stracey — who may have read Anne Gilchrist's enthusiastic 'A Woman's Estimate of Walt Whitman' (1870) — protested: 'Why say this? Walt Whitman would not agree with you.'

Theodore offers a fair enough summary of part of the argument of Bacon's essay 'Of Friendship' (1597–1612?) though the striking image of friendship opening a man's heart 'as an aperient would open his bowels' is not Bacon's at all. Bacon's statement was that 'No Receipt openeth the heart, but a true Friend.' Bacon probably knew Montaigne's essay 'Of Friendship' (1580) and, given Theodore's comment that 'I think it was a passage in Montaigne which finally turned my thoughts and habits to a life of contemplation' (October 23, 1936), we can be safe in assuming that Montaigne was to be numbered among 'the many wise men' who had something to say on the topic. Yet the thrust of Theodore Powys's essay is to repudiate mere 'friendship and the like' and to embrace Whitmanesque 'comradeship' and the brotherhood of man without quite understanding all that such 'adhesiveness' implied. The call for men to acknowledge 'strong laws' and 'leave false weakness behind' is, moreover, expressed in language that suggests an understandable — but happily short-lived — enthusiasm for Nietzsche's concept of 'overman', here more or less treated as a prerequisite to true brotherhood. John Cowper Powys, on the other hand, does not quibble about terminology and does not hesitate to affirm the value of unreconstructed friendship. In his essay on Montaigne (*Suspended Judgments*, 1923) he exclaims: 'But friendship — of the noble, rare, absolute kind such as existed between Montaigne and his sweet Etienne — is the only antidote, the only healing ointment, the only anodyne ...'(41).

Given that Theodore was never overly concerned with distinctions of genre, we need not worry too much about whether the 'stories' he sent to America with John in 1905, which were later passed on to Louis Wilkinson, were actually stories as such. 'Cheriton' is one of four items on similar paper in the Bissell Collection and tied in the same way with coloured thread. Even if we are willing to grant that the other three, 'Mary Aston', 'Jeremy Bird', and 'Moon Daisies', qualify as stories, 'Cheriton' surely does not. It is a vignette: a celebration of country life ('the earth-life') as pastoral in which we are offered the conventional participants in a kind of *tableau vivant* — the shepherd and his flock, the dairy maid calling the cow, and the barking dog on the farm. If the sentiments expressed in the piece are to be taken at face value, they present something of a puzzle. How can we reconcile the narrator's claim that the artist and the countryman share a common sensibility with our knowledge of Theodore's deeply disillusioning experience of country folk while he was a farmer in East Anglia, now fully revealed in *This Is Thyself*? Though he had not moved away from himself (and his abiding melancholy), by 1905 he had good reason to be content with life: an attractive young wife, a home of his own facing the village green, and an untested faith in his powers as a writer. Is there not a certain smugness — or is it bravado — in 'Let the world go dance on, I have my task' — a statement that also gives the whole piece something of the quality of a manifesto? At the same time, it is hard to see the essay as much more than an intellectual exercise. Claims such as 'All things can be wrought by the mind' and 'the world is as we wish it to be' suggest that it is also an exercise in wish-fulfilment.

J. Lawrence Mitchell

HRHRC = Harry Ransom Humanities Research Center

COMMENTARY 2

It is not always the most agreeable thing to eaves-drop on a writer learning their trade. Readers of Theodore Powys are not going to find untapped masterpieces beyond his published novels and short stories, of that we may be fairly certain. What we find confirms what is already known. Powys was a writer who focused on one central theme, what is potentially the huge theological issue of sin and redemption. He was drawn to the writings of the Christian mystics in his quest for a means of reconciling what seemed the irreconcilable instincts for good and evil that reside in human nature. This led him down the path of uncompromising honesty where the subject of sin was concerned;

he could never be satisfied with compromise, with the kind of gentility that swept uncomfortable truths under the carpet and preached appeasement. His was the stubborn honesty of William Blake:

> I was angry with my friend;
> I told my wrath, my wrath did end.
> I was angry with my foe;
> I told it not, my wrath did grow.

Powys's earliest published work shows him attempting to adopt the voice of a preacher, the role of an elder; and this creates all sorts of problems with working in a sustainable idiom, essentially because it is manifestly an assumed voice. It is not something that is coming naturally to his pen. The more one reads Powys's early work, the more it becomes apparent that the problems we encounter there are almost entirely to do with 'voice' rather than anything else; the ideas are pretty much in place from the first, and they changed very little throughout his writing life. In 'On A Future Life', addressed to 'Mr. Feeblemind' Powys's attempt to force his way into John Bunyan's manner results in at best an imitation that distracts from the central idea of reconciliation with death, and at worst a parody that slides towards whimsy, not to mention a distasteful tone of patronising self-righteousness:

> Man is part of earth and has lived since its beginning and will live until its end. Thus does philosophy help the strong, but it leaves the weak in an ill-taking. Now let us learn how to console the weak and save the poor feeble minds in despair.

This kind of thing had to go, it was an 'ill-taking' indeed! And of course Powys knew it had to go, and it did; though by no means all readers of *Innocent Birds* or *Unclay* have necessarily been over impressed by what replaced it!

For those of us that are, it remains intriguing to see Powys working through the implications of 'Friendship' as opposed to 'brotherhood' or 'comradeship'. Here we do well to remind ourselves that he is by no means exceptional in his reflections. In Book VI of *The Excursion*

Wordsworth describes how a Royalist and a Parliamentarian ('flaming Jacobite / And sullen Hanoverian') learned mutual respect and 'fellowship' within the neutral territory of a churchyard, a place where they were reminded of the common fate of all humanity. The near-by church is full of monuments and banners that describe a history of victors and vanquished framed in its telling by a political order that is rooted in the world this side of the grave, that is narrowly aligned with a worldly sense of propriety amenable to those who wield power in the temporal sphere. Powys too prefers to view the church from the churchyard:

> Man hath ever tried to escape the eternal laws of the universe. He has tried to bend the colossal wisdom of the destinies, to turn them aside, so that his own way may be sweet and his own path easy to traverse. To him the smooth way seemed ever the best, and the way of lies easy for his feet. Man finds the twisted way of shame easier than the strong hills of truth, for in high places truth lives and in a strong clear air.

There are compelling, challenging reasons why so much of Wordsworth's poetry takes place out of doors; it is about much more than a vague 'feel good factor' attached to nature worship; and Theodore Powys knew his Wordsworth well, he knew that Wordsworth's Nature was about far more than the poems which described scenic beauty and inward peace, he knew that this was only to be won with difficulty from 'the strong hills of truth'. Powys was also at one with many of his Romantic predecessors in looking with justified suspicion at the Church building when it was claimed as the dwelling place of the God who commands the 'high places' and the 'strong clear air'.

Readers of *Mr. Weston's Good Wine* still debating the status of Weston himself, will find a valuable clue in 'On God'. If Weston is God, what sort of a God is he? Now we know:

> Here in this island, with us who live in this age of iron, it seems that God rests, a commercial figure set in a cage of gold and hid in the midst of a cloud, His mind a strange medley of wrath,

> covetousness and doting fondness, His love the love of a young and foolish girl. The weakness of man hath desired this God, and has found him.

Weston is the God we choose to make him; should we object to certain traits in his character, we are criticising ourselves: 'we make Him a slave to our weakness, a pander to our lusts, a collector of our debts'; and Weston is all these things, as well as being — beyond those moments — utterly enigmatic and unknowable. No, the Mr. Weston of Theodore Powys's novel is no more God than is the Mr. Weston of Jane Austen's *Emma*, which is of course the point of Powys's reference.

What Powys needed to establish was a literary format that would enable him to gesture towards the God that was not Weston. At the point of writing these essays, he still had a good way to go. He shared the instincts of the Modernists of his time, delving once more into the Romantic literary tradition, and then pushing further back through the eighteenth century to what had come before that, in order to try and set the superficialities of the present, its materialism, its hedonism, to one side, and to look once more earthward for an answer: 'Better are the obscure and vulgar that worship wood and stone, for wood and stone have their hardness and strength, but this God is weak as a shadow.' But having got this far, and in this idiom, Powys was about to make a mess of it, and once he had made a mess of it, I doubt he needed anyone to tell him so:

> I asked once a wise man to explain and make clear this matter and he sent unto me out of his hut a little old woman with a great beard and scarce two teeth in her head, who spake thus unto me with signs.
>
> She dug a hole in the earth, and burying her head therein she seemed to listen for a good while, then she shook off the mould from her hair, and kissed the earth. And I knew that she desired to hide her thoughts in the earth where they might grow and I heard a voice that said 'Man is the soil, and not the plant, and the racecourse and not the runner. And he that finds his God must lose him.'

Reading this, we are able to appreciate more than ever, perhaps, Powys's achievement in the works of his literary maturity. Bizarre bearded women burying their heads in the earth disappear, to be replaced by Mr. Solly in *Innocent Birds* burying R. Mackenzie's *A History of America* in his back garden; to be replaced by the Revd Mr. Hayhoe finding that there is no more Jane Austen to read, 'Mr. Hayhoe sighed deeply. "*Pride and Prejudice* is finished," he said'; and replaced by Mr. Weston taking such pride in his *magnum opus*, but being prepared nevertheless to tamper with it. Referring to Psalm 104, he says, 'had I the proofs in my hands now I would certainly, when I think how much has been said against my writings, alter the last verse':

> 'I know what you would say,' said Luke, smiling; 'you would say, "Let the critics be consumed out of the earth!"'
>
> Mr. Weston nodded. He regarded Luke for a little in a most loving manner.

And a final replacement: most certainly better than the shamefully romanticised, commercialised description of 'Cheriton' is the bleak, unrelenting account of a loveless, depraved village community that we find starkly described in Chapter 13 of *Black Bryony*. This is Theodore Powys writing in the 1920s, so it is better, because it is worse; Powys's novels and short stories were the outcome of a long creative journey, in the course of which he had evolved a way of writing where he could bear to look on such brutality and cynicism with a steady eye, and attempt to communicate them to a readership in a style that had become his own unimpeded voice. As he himself says in 'On Friendship':

> Behold this strange wild voice has spoken truth, the little plants know it, the trees of the fields know, and the live animals understand.

John Williams

LLEWELYN POWYS

An Exile's Return

[Aug 2nd 1919] Arrived at Weymouth. I find my father much aged after my long exile in Africa. I understand now the full meaning of the Biblical phrase 'stricken in years'. Though still upright enough I notice a pathetic drag in his steps if he walks far, and his hands shake and he finds difficulty in laying hold of the right word.

In the afternoon walked with him across Lodmoor, I in a kind of frenzy pouring out stories about Africa — stories of natives, and lions, and bush fires — which seem so exciting to my mind now against this homely Dorset background.

A bed made up for me in the garden within a stone's throw of the sea. Here I try to sleep but in reality await in a kind of ecstasy the coming of the dawn. At the first indications of light over the sea, a number of black birds fly heavily past — cormorants coming into the backwater from their roosting places along the shore by the White Nore — coming in to sit all day on the black posts by the edge of the inland water, waiting for fish. Presently the sun is high above the horizon, the whole front glitters in its light, the rounded window panes of the old Georgian houses shining like sheets of silver — and another seaside day begins. There is a stir in the house behind and my brother and sister come out for their morning bathe. I feel about me a delicious atmosphere of holidays, with the breakfast table all ready laid and all so different from Africa.

Aug 4th At 11 a.m. I and my brother [Bertie] to the quay and away by steamer to Lulworth Cove. Sunshine upon the bay. We sit on a coil of ropes in the stern of the little vessel. I listen to his stories of the War — stories of desperate bewildered fighting amongst rusty barbed-wire and how in the end he came home bribing a soviet council with pieces of soap — and how he came down the Rhine in a steamer and

Llewelyn Powys in 1919,
taken just before he left Africa for England.
(photograph by courtesy of Peter Foss)

how his friend for a pound of nuts embraced a German girl amongst some barrels at some little town where the steamer stopped. From Lulworth we set out for East Chaldon to the home of brother Theodore, I overjoyed to feel the soft sod of these chalk downs under my feet again. The very smell of the bracken and brambles of these English hedgerows like a cool soothing draft to my fretted nerves — so utterly different from the astonishing and insidious tropical scenes I have been used to for so many years. Met [Theodore] resting in a sheltered valley — a handkerchief by his side full of cold mushrooms. We kissed each other and sat talking. There was a tremor in his rich well-modulated voice and as we three lay resting there I kept watching his face which had altered much — the face of a high priest worshipping at an altar, deserted by man and God — an infinite sadness in his eyes which are so overhung by his forehead, and his hair already almost white. I think at the birth of a child one might well pray 'Let not the child be found in the gates of wisdom — let it not seek God' .

After lunch walked back to the stone circle. Taking tea at The Plough Inn where was excellent butter and fresh eggs and all served in the bar. God! I was glad to be in such a place again, surrounded by barrels of beer and cider and good wholesome tavern smells.

Aug 7th A very gay family next door who bathe every day — one of them a young girl of fifteen, slim and tall and pretty, but with rather too shrill a voice.

Aug 8th To Yetminster by train and motor to Sherborne — a tennis party there, the garden brilliant with red geraniums, a little [?] there very merry and cheerful — 50 years old and evidently not much concerned with God. Extraordinary to me that these people can be content to let their lives glide by occupied thus. Can't they hear the old Abbey bells registering the passing of time — the passing away of these choice precious hours of consciousness in a world so imaginative and dramatic? Haven't they the trick to see it? I wore my African veldt hat and felt curiously separated from these folk. 'Why Powys,' said one of them, 'you look like Sir Philip Sidney — some old Elizabethan adventurer like Sir Philip Sidney.' And in truth my mood was the mood of such a one.

Aug 9th Weymouth again and to church with my father. To St

Luke's church — a terribly vulgar place, deplorable in appearance both without and within. I liked to hear the beautiful and familiar prayers again and liked looking at pretty Nelly Blake who sat opposite. But Lord! to think that this kind of thing still continues. I seemed to get into the minds of these disgusting good old men — with their Sunday garments and oiled white hair, could see them expecting to obtain some extraordinary kind of existence after death in reward for their present regular and sombre devotions [. . . .] I felt as if the whole congregation was made up of grocers and drapers and successful commercial travellers — only such people I thought could have tolerated such a service — these soft hassocks, pew mats, hymnbook boxes seemed to smother and stifle you — devastating, most horrible.

Watched my little next door neighbour bathing — a very pretty figure, but these bathing dresses are invariably ugly. I was surprised and interested to see how developed she was — her breasts as round and full as a woman's.

Aug 10th By train to near Woking — a nice house and the B's attractive people. Little Kathleen in the costume of an Indian welcomed me at the door. All very well appointed and liked listening to [his] stories of people he had met — Ruskin, Morris, Pater, Arnold. One afternoon we drove to Sutton Court [Place], an old country house belonging to the Duke of Sutherland — a very stately Tudor building of red brick. I found a tiny miniature of Rabelais under a glass case in the library — a curiously religious face with long straggling beard and dark eyes, haggard, ecstatic.

The garden very lovely — wide sweeping lawns bordered by dazzling flower beds, and behind tiny sun-warmed enclosures with summer houses and fish ponds. Walked back but was too conscious of the nearness of London to really enjoy it — motor bicycles and motor cars continually passing and the trees blackened by smoke.

Up to London and to [Bernie's] where I find Louis Wilkinson — much merry talk — and I chagrined that time should have made so little mark on him. I find him as debonair and irrepressible as ever.

With [Bernie] to Shepperton, looking for rooms. Find an excellent tavern The King's Head with garden running down to the river — lunch is prepared for us under a mulberry tree and we hardly sat to it but down comes the rain and everything has to be carried [in]. I like the place which suits well — we both liked it — we liked the old woman in the kitchen and thought the servant girl Effy a very sweet creature. We had hoped to get to Laleham to see Matthew Arnold's grave but there was no time. I like the place and will not easily forget my first view of it — with its green drenched garden running down to the Thames — looking so old, so hidden away, so Shakespearean — full, one would fancy, of rue and a thousand simples. It had a very distinct and definite atmosphere of its own.

Aug 18th In the afternoon went out with Louis — went to the Burlington Arcade and to the Bristol, but I could not interest myself in these town trots — they seemed to me sinister and I suspected them all [of] having the pox. 'Goodnight,' I heard one say, as we edged past her towards the door, and the whispered salutation seemed like the little midnight vice become articulate.

Aug 19th At night went to Bertie's office in Adelphi — a very quaint old-fashioned quarter of the city — any number of Queen Anne houses. Walked back to West Kensington together and began to understand a little the mysterious beauty and attractiveness of London at night time — the very passing of life's stream made audible, the sound of it like a great river and with vistas, illumined paths, dusk glades, shadowy places on each bank. Indeed we came upon just such a retreat, and even its appropriate deity — a stone fountain, carved after the form of a woman in Portland stone — a thing of real value and known to my brother for many years past, as it stands just here out of the pell mell and with grass and trees about it.

Aug 20th To dinner with Squire at Swan House. A lovely upper room with countless bookshelves and many old tomes. I had not seen him since Cambridge days. I liked him. Is it something feline that one notices as he moves so softly across the carpet? Or is it an owl sleepy but ready to pierce the vitals of rat or mouse in a moment of time?

He has just the expression he always did have, only of course his personality being more developed one becomes more conscious of it — those dreamy, yet vividly awake eyes make one feel curiously uneasy when they rest on you for a moment — a devilish clever fellow certainly and possibly a great poet, but I wish he had not told me he was a good Christian and thought very highly of G. K. Chesterton.

Aug 21st To Shepperton. My cousin Ralph and his daughter and my friend Bernie — we go for a walk after lunch to countryside different from what I am used to — very flat.

In the evening [Bernie] and I to the lock and then sit and watch the moonlight on the Thames and the shadows of the seven poplars — and a red light from some upper window in a mysterious building opposite — 'the witch girl's window'. We talk much of *Wolf's-Bane*, and I declare it to be a volume full of great and inspired poetry — a volume that cannot fail to live. But then, he says, why does Squire think little of it and also Louis Wilkinson? Squire's taste I suspect as being too technical and think it quite conceivable that he would miss really great poetry if he was put off by slovenly workmanship. Louis Wilkinson of course is jealous [....], a mean yapping jealousy of a commonplace kind before real genius.

Aug 30th I have had really no time to write my diary — have been on the river all day and every day.

The most wonderful weather — moonlight and lapping water — lapping water and bright sunshine — cool clear transparent depths — flashing kingfishers, watercress, poplar trees and cows in late summer pastures.

Aug 31st To Laleham and into the churchyard to look for Matthew Arnold's grave. We found it. The place is marked by a white Italian tombstone — terribly cheap and garish, the letters not even cut out. It might have shown the burial place of any Victorian tradesman. But there was something of his spirit still brooding over the place — over smooth flowing waters of the Thames, over the cedar trees and wide flat harvest fields.

Sept 1st Down to Horsebridge in Hampshire, where I stay in an old mill by the side of the river Test — a tangled overgrown garden behind ... a fine pear tree with the ripe and clean fruit all about on the ground and a great many wasps.

Sept 4th Back again at Weymouth. In the evening I wandered up to the town and along St Thomas's Street. It was the same. I could see no change, the same narrow curved appearance and the same indefinable suggestion of some inland town not near the sea at all. I stood on the old bridge looking towards the backwater, the water washing back under the arches — on my left the red blinds of The Fisherman's Return threw a warm light on to the narrow street. I looked at the old quaint bow windows and they seemed to represent the very body of that romance which hangs over ancient seafaring ports — these little dusty semi-circular windows must have listened, so one fancies, to the returning foot-tread of a thousand seamen home at last from distant countries with strange trophies in their pockets and strange tales in their heads. Weymouth harbour — I liked to think of it here still keeping even Dorset in touch with the great outer world so that a man can leave Cerne Abbas or Stalbridge, let us say, and travel to France or the other side of the earth without setting foot in another county. The water lapped its way seaward, a small rain began falling, the pavements shone. Honest soldiers with simple faces and country accents loafed past with their girls. I listened to their talk, their very oaths falling on my ears like benedictions.

Sept 14th I have acquired a revolving shelter and today I went along the coast looking for some suitable position where I can put it up — some position on the coast where I shall not be disturbed, and where I shall be able to possess my soul again during the long winter months. I did not search in vain — at the very top of a hill some three hundred yards from the sea stands an old ruined cottage with a little deserted garden round it enclosed by low stone walls. As soon as I saw it I knew it to be the place for me — a desolate haunted garden with long wavy dry grass and a few old-fashioned flowers, and a deep open well and goblin ash tree and all in sound and sight of the sea and overlooked by this thatched dilapidated cottage — with the appearance of a skull.

Sept 15th Visited the farmer and got leave to put my shelter in the cottage garden.

Sept 20th Slept in my shelter for the first time — was waked by a shepherd and had some good talk with him about country matters. He likes me. His father is over 80 but still looks after sheep somewhere near Cranborne Chase and he can just remember selling hurdles with his grandfather who was of the same trade.

Sept 30th To Sutton Poyntz, a little village under the downs, and here I came upon an old eighteenth century sundial let into a delicious

Poxwell Stone-Circle, Dorset.

A frequent trysting place for the Powyses, and particularly sacred to Llewelyn and Theodore; often mentioned in Llewelyn's essays and unpublished writings from 1911 onwards.

(photograph by Shelagh Powys, 2000)

red brick wall with the words 'Life is a shadow' written underneath it. I wondered what old village philosopher was responsible for these emphatic words. I like them very well.

Oct 15th Tonight as I came up to my hut at 11 p.m. I saw a halo in the sky to the right when I had climbed to the top of the field. I saw the light come from Jupiter just risen over the horizon. I enjoy the most wonderful nights in this place and already I feel as if I am shaking off the deadly influence of Africa. If the wind is in the west I turn my hut towards the coastline — so that I can see the sun rise over by St Alban's Head. I also like watching the waves breaking against the rocks by Redcliffe Bay, which has such a lonely deserted air during these autumn months.

In the evening I get a glimpse sometimes of the West Bay between the hills of Abbotsbury — a silver line of water.

Nov 5th The first hard frost. The ground hard as iron.

Nov 6th I got up this morning at 4 o'clock and with my satchel over my shoulder set out for East Chaldon.

Cold as the devil, a full moon in the sky. I passed through the village of Preston with the stillness of night upon it — only the sound of my footsteps on the hard white road, the cottages on both sides quite silent as it has been at daily recurring intervals since the earliest time. I stood outside The Plough Inn and listened to a clock striking, it was the only sound which indicated the presence of human beings — otherwise all muffled up and silent as it might have been a thousand years ago. When I passed the stone circle I saw towards the east the first glow of the approaching dawn. By West Chaldon Farm a blackbird came screaming out of the hedge — and under the thatch in a tiny dormer window I saw a light — a servant doubtless already astir. A little further on I met a labourer. By the time I reached the gate of my brother's house dawn had broken.

Today I finished my essay on Bewick. Surely in my present abode I must have caught the spirit and genius of the old north countryman — the ash tree and gaunt ruined house look down on me as I write.

Nov 15th I like very well my night walks to and from Weymouth, the sea on one hand and on the other Lodmoor. A white milestone with 11 miles to Wareham written upon it. And an old turnpike house white-washed and with a very romantic weather-beaten appearance.

I also often see the bended figures of the fishermen against the sky on the beach above me, as they haul in their nets.

Christmas Eve Woke feeling curiously depressed because of this wretched damp weather or because of the season and the memory of the past at Montacute when we would all be at home at this time.

In the evening I left the house and went off to The Fisherman's Return and sat there till late drinking beer.

Jan 1st [1920] A cold day — we walked to Portland Bill and watched the waves there breaking upon the rocks and in the caves to the right. My mind all the time full of Hardy and his genius — 'The Souls of the Slain' and passages from *The Well-Beloved* where he describes the funeral of the girl, the coffin borne by six bearers moving to the church like an animal with 12 legs and a glimpse of a ship at sea seen underneath. We saw a brig beating round the island.

Jan 2nd News comes of a ship wrecked on the Kimmeridge and 40 sailors drowned — doubtless the very one we saw yesterday. They called at Portland and asked for a pilot to take them up the channel, but there was no pilot and they set out again only to founder on Kimmeridge Ledge two hours later. I know those ledges with dead man's pool behind. There is something strangely thrilling and awful when one thinks of this ship back from India and then to meet disaster at the very end of the journey.

Jan 4th To Evershot by train and walked to Sherborne — along the road from High Stoy.

I came first to Lion's Gate, a tiny hamlet. An old woman stood at her door. I asked her how many miles it was to Sherborne. While we were talking I was conscious of the sound of a man's voice in the cottage as though some monotonous reading was going on. It was, she told me, her husband John Napier — a woodcutter now eighty years old and bedridden with rheumatism [who] would now never cease day or night from this strange monologue. 'But what does he talk about?' I asked. He talks, she said, of his past work of felling trees and cutting brushwood and binding faggots. Presently I continued my journey but it took me a long time before I could rid my mind of the idea of the old man whose mind and body had been so contorted by his labour. The way led through Middlemarsh — the ditches were full of water, orchards on each side of the road. I thought of the caravan tracks I was used to in Africa — of the dust and heat of the plains. I walked on and on, tireless and exuberant — the milestones were left behind one after another. Presently the sun went down, seen for the last time, a round ball of red fire behind some tall elm trees — the bare branches showing against the light like pieces of spread-out sea-weed.

I came to woods and places I knew. I remembered the bluebells of the copse on my right and the old church tower where I had once found an owl's nest on a far off summer afternoon.

An odd shaped conveyance took form in front of me. When I overtook it, it turned out to be a cider maker journeying to Sherborne with all the things that belonged to his trade being drawn along. I drifted down West Hill with him as a companion. When we had passed that part of the road overshadowed by the Honeycombe Woods I got my first glimpse of the town. I could see the lights in the school buildings — lights warm, festive and familiar. In a few minutes I was passing Dancing Hill, had crossed the bridge over the Yeo and was advancing up the well-known streets. Far above me towered the great Abbey — from its massive darkness came the sound of the clock striking the hour.

Jan 20th Every day I see slight indications of the approach of spring. There is something very wistful and winning and childlike about such tokens — something that makes one catch one's breath. Certainly Europe is the place to understand the mythology of the Greeks — spring represented as a girl let loose reluctantly by the sullen earth.

I see in the copse below my hill that the willows are crowned with their delightful little furry buds — and I find snowdrops scattered on the Osmington road by the National School and each morning when I come down to breakfast there are blackbirds singing in the little back garden behind Greenhill Terrace.

COMMENTARY

When John Cowper Powys said in a letter of 14 August 1936 to Kenneth Hopkins that Llewelyn's 'early writings — and in one sense all his writings — were based on his early diaries' he was thinking not only of *Skin for Skin* but of the many 'simulated' or made-up diary extracts which Llewelyn composed in the period 1912 to 1920, utilising material from his real diaries or simply assembling events in his recent past which he put into diary form. On the successful publication of 'A Consumptive's Diary' by John Squire in 1914 (*The New Statesman*, 7 March 1914) and 'Africa' by A. R. Orage in 1915 (*The New Age*, 8 July 1915), Llewelyn had realised that there was a market for such 'diary' pieces, and that editors found them appealing and useful material even when there was no obvious shape or narrative content. They were also easy to contrive, to edit and alter. Consequently Llewelyn penned a number of these simulated diaries in an attempt to break into the writing trade, several of them remaining unpublished, including the example above.

'An Exile's Return' is my title for an untitled MS 'diary' which was drafted into a diary pocket book for 1912, but which dates from 1920. This pocket book, marked by Alyse Gregory as 'No.15' was used as a notebook after the Great War and contains other material, including the original of 'Black Gods'. It is now part of the Bissell Gift in the Powys Society Collection at the Dorset County Museum. It is important from an archival point of view to note that Llewelyn often used spare diaries as notebooks in which to draft essays, and to be aware therefore that a distinction has to be made between the date of the diary used and the date of the material in it.

This piece takes up the story of Llewelyn's return from Africa in 1919, as given in another simulated diary, 'A Sheepman's Diary' which first appeared in *The Dial* in April 1920 (republished in *Ebony and Ivory* in 1923). Llewelyn had drafted that shortly after he had returned from Africa in August 1919, and had offered it to Squire (possibly at the meeting described in 'An Exile's Return' — see Elwin, 139 and *Letters*, 102). 'A Sheepman's Diary' had ended with Llewelyn landing at Southampton on 2 August 1919 and returning home to

Montacute, an impossibility since his father, Revd C. F. Powys, had retired from his living at Montacute and had moved to 3 Greenhill Terrace, Weymouth. This in itself should be a warning that the events described in these simulated diaries have to be treated with some caution. Dates, for example, cannot be relied upon biographically, for frequently they were thrown together in order to give the appearance of a sensible sequence of time. Llewelyn also disguised names, with an eye to publication; for example in 'An Exile's Return', Bernard Price O'Neill is referred to as 'Dr Fingal Roughty', Ralph Shirley as 'R', and Theodore sometimes as 'my hermit brother'.

Since the MS is a raw draft I have intervened somewhat to tidy up the text, which indeed is what happened when these 'diaries' were published. Punctuation has been modified, and names of persons restored. There are several small omissions, chiefly one which simply elaborates Llewelyn's attack on the congregation of St Luke's, and another which mentions several of Louis Wilkinson's books (such as *The Buffoon*) as proof of his jealousy of JCP. This simulated diary account can be compared with the essay called 'A West Countryman's Return', which was published in *The Countryman* (Autumn 1956). The provenance and authority of that piece is open to question because of the nature of its publication — sent, according to the editor of the magazine, 'in an old manuscript book found among the writer's papers ... by his widow'. 'A West Countryman's Return' reads as though it is an essay paraphrase of part of the diary extract, written possibly as an alternative version when Llewelyn became disillusioned with the diary format. In any event it complements the version above, and can usefully be read in conjunction with it (see *The Powys Journal* vii, 1997, 202–6).

Peter J. Foss

Llewelyn Powys
The Essayist at Work: Letters to H.G.Tavender

Compiled with an Introduction by Peter J. Foss

In 1983 I was given a batch of papers which included fourteen letters which Llewelyn Powys had written from Chydyok, Chaldon Herring, to Henry George Tavender (*c.* 1863–1936). The letters dated from between November 1935 and March 1936, up to just before H. G.Tavender's death in Bournemouth at the age of 73. The archive (now part of the Powys Society Collection at the Dorset County Museum) included the draft of an Obituary written by Llewelyn Powys for Tavender, which I have no evidence was published.

Henry George Tavender had been a stone mason of Montacute (living at Fernside) in the 1890s. He had moved to Yeovil in the early 1900s where his occupation was given as 'stone mason and merchant' in the 1906 Directory, and his address as Addlewell Lane and 5 Park Street. By the time of the First World War he had become owner of the Ham Hill Quarry and glove factory, and was a leading Baptist figure in the community, his family being well known to all the Powyses.

In 1935 Llewelyn renewed acquaintance with him in the course of his research on the Montacute poet and musician Thomas Shoel (1759–1823). The following correspondence, of which only one of the letters is from Tavender, displays something of the conscientiousness with which Llewelyn went about garnering information for his country essays of the 1930s. He made use both of standard works and local records, often lent to him by friends or borrowed by friends from libraries or inspected by them in national archives. He also went to some trouble to collect *viva voce* information, local folk-memory and family history. He sent copies of his drafts to acquaintances to check details, and to his brothers for their opinions.

In all it was a remarkable endeavour for a man who, in the 1930s, was mostly ill and invalided, but relied of course upon the good will and labour of friends and connections. It shows something of the respect in which Llewelyn was held, both as writer and as 'a son of Montacute' — and son of the former vicar — that many people were willing to aid his research so thoroughly. The essays that emerged from these years were many of them significant records of country life and oral memory and as such have a place in our national archive in much the same fashion as the work of Thompson and Sturt.

The collection is headed by a letter from Dr Wyndham Goodden, an M.D. and spare-time photographer who provided many of the photographs for Llewelyn's two West Country collections, *Dorset Essays* (1935) and *Somerset Essays* (1937). It is addressed from Weyside Cottage, Upwey, Weymouth, and dated 22 August 1935. It must have been sent by Llewelyn to Tavender for interest and failed to be returned. The graveyard referred to is that at Five Ashes, Odcombe, a non-conformist cemetery, and the resultant photograph was published in *Somerset Essays*, opposite p.133, to accompany the eventual publication of the essay on 'Thomas Shoel':

My dear Powys,

I return Tilly Coles' letter and have made note of her address and Mrs Greenham. I hope you will be well enough before the autumn to do the Montacute trip with me, accompanied of course by Mrs Powys — you would require to do nothing but sit in the car and those people could come out and talk to you.

I shall be going to Taunton on the 26th to return the books and will then get the works of T. Shoel if they are there. If I cannot work in Martock on the same day I will write to Mr Saunders and make the enquiries about Cromwell and the graveyard. My sister says she has never heard of Shoel or a new Baptist church, but I can find out all about it next time I am in Montacute. ... Probably I shall take Montacute *en route* to Taunton and could then run up to the graveyard and get a photograph. Do you think the gate is kept locked? With our very kind regards, Yours sincerely, Wyndham C. Goodden. P.S. I do not want the two prints again.

The sequence of Tavender letters begins in November 1935 (the date of the first; most of the others remain undated), and refers to correspondence with a great-grand-daughter of Thomas Shoel. The Mr Burt of the letter was the son of Julia Burt, née Shoel, Thomas Shoel's youngest daughter:

[*printed*] Chydyok
Chaldon Herring,
Dorchester, Dorset

November 1935

Dear Mr Tavender,

Mrs Wilton of Townend, Montacute, has suggested that I write to you to ask if you know anything about her great grandfather, Thomas Shoel, the poet. I pray you to let me know even the least scrap of hearsay you may remember about him. I have been very interested by some of his poems — especially the shorter ones that are less influenced by his contemporaries. He must have been a very remarkable man, as sensitive as a leaf and a true poet. I cannot imagine why we were never told about him, but you chapel people were often ahead of the church in culture of the purest sort. I would have liked to have persuaded you to visit me, but Mr Burt seemed to think that such an expedition would be more than you could undertake and as I have been in bed for over two years we are not likely to see each other again. [... .]

Was Thomas Shoel buried in the churchyard or at Five Ashes? Had Julia Burt any sisters? In what house or part of the village did Shoel live? Who was Caleb Shoel? Do you remember any Shoels? The tiniest scrap of information would be of great interest to me. I send you the loyal greeting of one Montacutian to Another. I can see your brother so well standing in the Borough. Yours sincerely, Llewelyn Powys. [P.S.] I am glad to say they have all of Shoel's works at the British Museum.

The first four letters of the batch are all replies to Tavender's detailed and ruminatory responses and are all written on printed headed paper, and were sent presumably in November and December 1935 when Llewelyn was finalising his essay, among others, about the Baptist minister Henry Hardin, which he knew would be of particular interest to his correspondent.

Dear Mr Tavender,

Thank you very much indeed for your valuable letter. It is very good of you to take such trouble and I was absorbed by every word of it. I am glad to know the site of the old chapel and very interested to hear your theory as to where Shoel lived and all your stories interest me very much. I cannot understand how it came about that we never were told of him. I know my mother would have been utterly entranced by his poetry and his musical inspirations.

It was good of you to think of lending me this charming little book [a copy of *The Life Beautiful*]. I am taking you at your word and will keep it for a few days. I was very sorry to read of your trouble with your eyes. I sympathise very much — my distemper has affected my optical nerves so that I can hardly read any length of time. If I get better I will try to come to see you, but this will not be till next summer. I eagerly await your next installment. Yours sincerely, Llewelyn Powys

My dear Mr Tavender,

I was very interested by your letter. Thank you for it. In a recent *John Bull* there was an 'exposure' of a Charles Geard who has been for many years a religious leader of some kind. I would like to hear whether you remember anything about him. He called himself Shiloh, the Messiah, and makes extravagant claims. He looks a little too smooth for my liking but he must be an interesting man in his way.

I understand that Shoel used to sit on Miles Hill so that he could look down Middle Street when he wrote his hymns and anthems. I am sending you many relevant papers on Shoel which I thought you might be interesting to you [*sic*] and might suggest to your mind new information. Please let me have them back again in a few days when you have looked them over. My sister was so pleased with your messages and I was told to send you renewed salutations. Yours very sincerely, Llewelyn Powys.

Dear Mr Tavender,

Thank you very much for your long interesting letter. I take it 'swine's wine' referred to black pudding — a favourite food of our

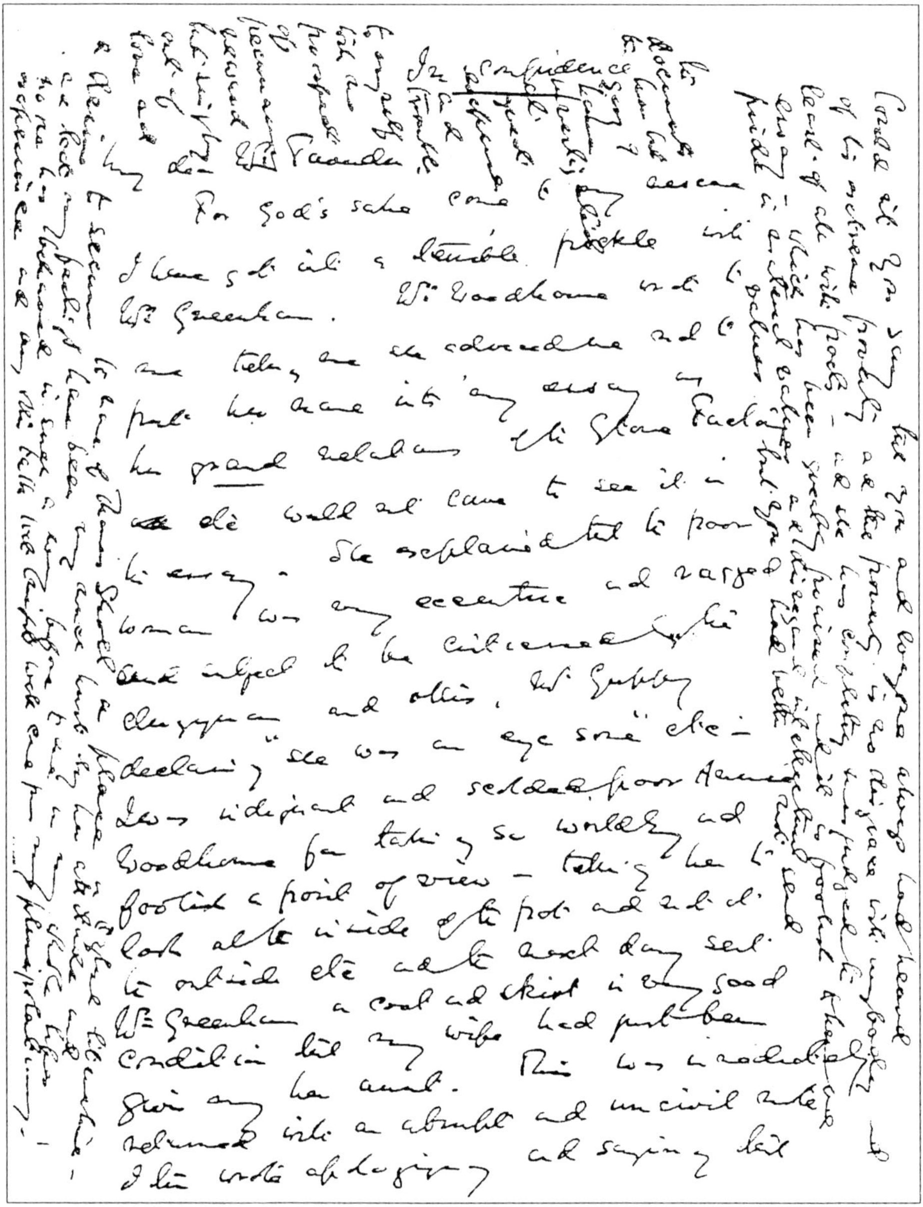
In confidence [illegible] Tavender

For God's sake come to [illegible]

I have got into a terrible pickle with Mr Woodhouse and Mr Greenham. [illegible]

[illegible] the Stone [illegible] grand [illegible] would not come to see it [illegible] She [illegible] the poor [illegible] my essay [illegible] eccentric and ragged woman [illegible] and others. [illegible] clergyman [illegible] "she was an eye sore" [illegible] declaring [illegible] was indignant and scolded poor [illegible] Woodhouse for taking so worldly and foolish a point of view — telling him to look at the inside of the pot and not at the outside [illegible] Mr Greenham a coat and skirt in very good condition that my wife had just been giving my aunt. This [illegible] an abrupt and uncivil note [illegible] and saying that I then wrote apologizing [illegible]

One of Llewelyn Powys's letters to H. G. Tavender, February/March 1936 (see p.56),

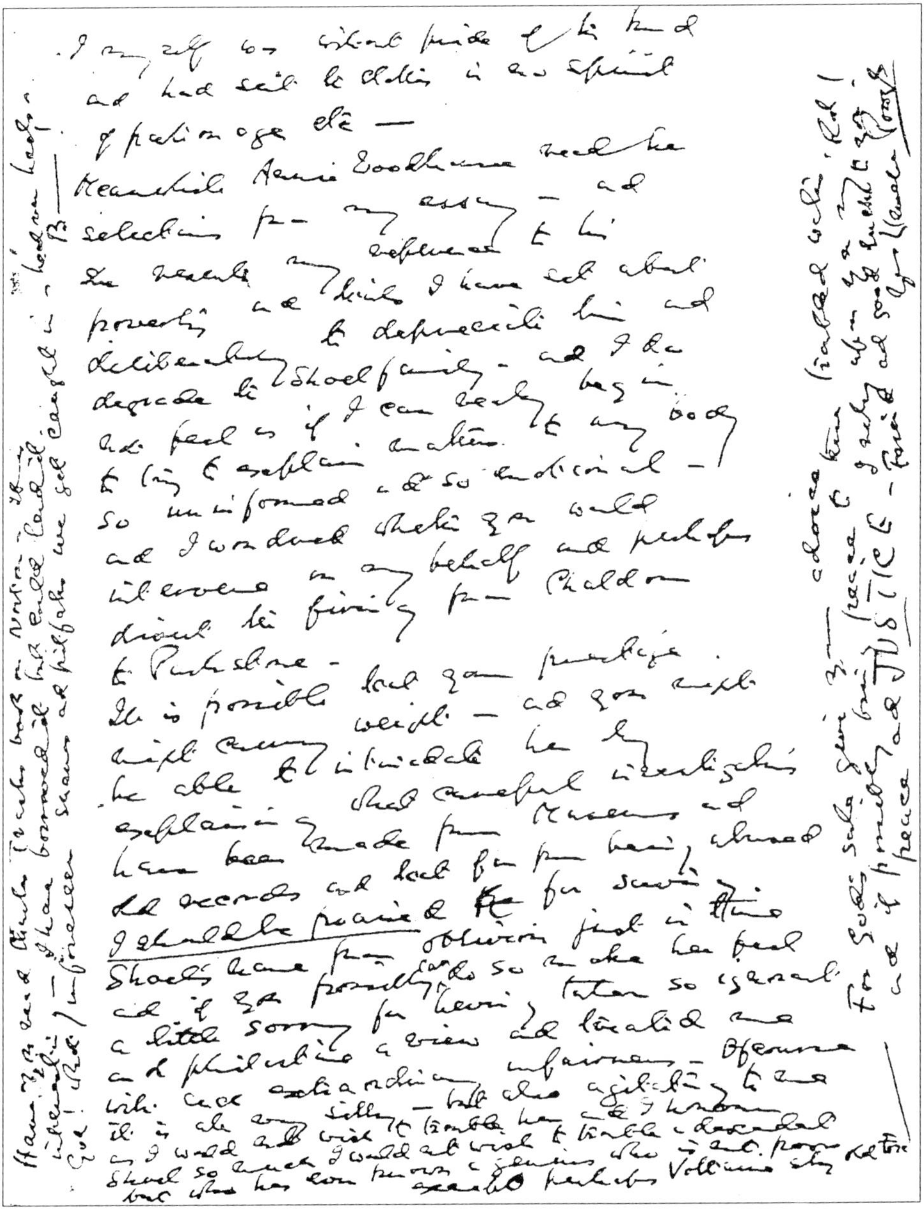

declaring he '<u>should be praised</u> for saving Shoel's name from oblivion'.

villagers! I think the behaviour of that roguish preacher unpardonable. With regard to the music of Shoel being at Taunton Museum I will make enquiries when I next see Dr Goodden. I did not ask him to worry his head about the music as the poetry was what I required.

I have heard from Mr Hardin's grandson — Mr William Osbourne, who tells me that somebody has told him that Shoel was born at Norton and spent his childhood there and returned to that village at the end of his life. I very much doubt the authenticity of his hearsay as his reference to Norton is casual in his Miles Hill poem and I think you or Ellen Greenham would have heard a rumour of it. Shoel speaks of a Robert Chaffey of Norton as having befriended him which suggests he was in touch with the village but I cannot believe he lived there. I have gone through the proofs of the Hardin essay and you shall have a copy when it comes out. Yrs. Ll. Powys.

The following letter — with a date of 'Jan 14 1936' handwritten by Tavender at the top left hand corner — was the first sent not on headed paper, and refers to the essay on Montacute House — called 'An Old English House' — which had appeared in the Atlantic Monthly *(CLV, No.5) for April 1935. It is followed by the reply given it by Tavender in a copy made by him and which therefore represents the only letter by Tavender in the batch, giving some idea of the detail and colour of the correspondent's information:*

[Jan 14 '36]

Dear Mr Tavender,

I was very pleased to get your last letter with its valuable enclosure. Thank you for the trouble you have taken. How charming his habit was of naming his tunes after the places where they were composed — Abbey Farm, Woodhouse etc. — I think Coombe Fountain must refer to the spring under Batemoor. Can you confirm this or was it perhaps the watercress pool in Pitt Pond wood? When I have my rough draft ready of my essay, you shall be the first to see it.

I am sending you also an essay of mine on Montacute House, my early memories of it, which I thought may interest you. Would you be careful to send it back as it is *my only copy*. My brother ARP made himself merry over the dialect of John Hanne — saying it was incorrect from first to last. As I am proposing to include this piece in my new book of *Somerset Essays* I wondered whether you could possibly get the dialect correct — on another piece of paper so that I could alter my mistakes. I should be most grateful for any hints you could give. Dr Goodden remembers his father telling him the squire John Phelips used to speak broad Somerset and used to say 'my name is Philips'. Philip was the pet name for a sparrow, and this may explain the bird heads on his shield. My sister wishes to thank you very much for your kind letter to her. Yours sincerely, Llewelyn Powys.

16/1/36 42 Alexandra Road,
Parkstone, Dorset

Dear Mr Powys,

I thank you for your letter and for the magazine which I will return in a few days. I have been interested in reading your essay on Montacute House, interested also in the house itself. During the earlier part of Lord Curzon's lease I did something in nearly all the main rooms and had men there on and off from 1915 to 1920. One thing was to open up the 8 blocked up windows inside the long Gallery. 8 three-light windows opened up on the side let in some daylight. I had about 25 to 30 tons of stone & mortar to get down from the gallery and it was fortunate that there was a luggage lift there. The John Phelips you mention had, about the year 1797, the cross tie beams which were connected with and held the wood principals cut off and then the stone roof tiles caused the roof to sag with serious results. Interest may also be found in the 'Skimmity riding' panel in Northern end of Great Hall. Lord Curzon had his own and the Phelips' coats-of-arms & family mottoes in Silk flags hung at the other end of the hall, Curzon motto being, 'Let Curzon hold what Curzon held'. I had heard of the legend concerning the 'Flaming cradle'. The version I heard said that one of the daughters of the family had an illegitimate child, and the others were so humiliated and angry that they put the child in the cradle, set fire to it and left the baby to burn. The facts somehow leaked out with the result as you give it.

In regard to the dialect and your brother's criticism, ask him 'try his hand' at it and see whether it is an easy job to write down dialect without making it somewhat conventional and yet keeping the meaning clear to ordinary readers. I will make a slight alteration or two on a separate piece of paper and you will then see that there is not much the matter with your version. Are you interested in 'Dialect', and if so have you any of Walter Raymond's books re. Somerset — or John Read's (a Somerset lad now Professor of Chemistry at St Andrews) or Dan'l Graingers 'Down-along Talks' etc etc. If you are interested and have none of such books I can lend you several if you care to have them, and if you let me know will send one or two with the 'Atlantic' when I return it. They are very good of their kind, the dialect and humour very interesting to those who care for it.

Re. Combe Fountain. It is possible that your suggestion that the name derives from the spring on the side of the slope running down from Batemoor Barn to the old flaxpit in Batemoor and which is called 'Batemoor spring'. I have in one or two of my old MSS music books a tune called 'Batemoor' or 'Batemore', also tunes named Hamdon Hill, Norton Field, Stoke, Yeovil, and other local names. But I have been unable to find any evidence of their being Shoel's. I am not competent to judge from their form, construction or style whether they are Shoel's. This perhaps could be settled by anyone trained in musical theory and construction.

The story of Nancy Cooper (or Cupper as she was more often called) was a sad and sordid one but I do not know the origin of it. She had two daughters and one son Tom, who went to Street near Glastonbury and made good, I believe. The other daughter's name was Harriet but better known as Curdly (Curly) Cupper, as when a young woman she had long curls. She married a neighbour named James Hann (Jim Warrior). Had some sons who when they grew up got work at Tintinhull and after the husband's death went there to live, and so far as I know are there now, except perhaps the mother (Curly). Did you know that Nancy had a husband living at Montacute? It was a mixed up lot in Middle St. Montacute, when I was a boy and collectively they had the nickname (if I may so call it) of 'The Royal Family'.

I began writing to you yesterday, but in the middle of it someone called on important business and stopped it. This partly explains why I have not acknowledged earlier receipt of letter and book and I trust you will excuse me. I thank you very much for your offer to send me rough draft of your essay on Shoel when ready. I shall [be] very pleased to have it, if it causes you no inconvenience to let me have it so early.

I am hoping you will get this tomorrow, but it may be Saturday when you get it. Trusting that your sisters are well and that you are standing up well to this very trying weather. I am yours sincerely, H. G. Tavender.

[*page of dialect notes*]

Dialect in 'An Old English House'

Yours: 'To mind 'em of it for everlasting.'

As I expect John Hann said it: 'To mind 'em o'et vur everlastin'.'

Yours: 'My granfer would say "God Almighty will shift em for it, maybe in thy time, may be in thy childers time, but sure as day comes he'll unroosty 'em".'

As John said it I expect: 'My granfer 'ood zay, "God a'mighty'll shift 'em vor et, maybe (probably 'mid be') in thy time, may be (mid-be?) in thee childerns time but sure as day da come he'll unroosty 'em".' (Mid-be for 'might be')

I knew 5 John Hanns in Montacute at one time but you could have known only 2 of them and possibly only one. These two would be John Hann the Builder and Quarry owner and John Hann, his carter, who used to go with horse & waggon with the worked stone for miles around. I think the latter must be the John you refer to. The former had a son John who died before his father. Apart from that none of them were related to each other. His carter, John, died in that part of Townend leading out to the back houses in 'Abbey' as it was called, beside John Hann senr's yard and stables. Was that the one you spoke to? H.G.T.

Llewelyn, despite the assurance in the following letter, never got round to altering John Hann's words in the re-publication of 'An Old English House' as 'Montacute House' in Somerset Essays. *Perhaps he might have done had it not been for his going to Switzerland in November 1936 when papers may have been left behind. In any case, Tavender had said that there was 'not much the matter' with Llewelyn's version. The publication of Llewelyn's essay 'The Rev. Henry Hardin (1838–1934)' in* The Congregational Quarterly *XIV, No.1 in January 1936 brought about the other contact referred to in this letter, and Hardin, the son, was to visit Llewelyn at Chydyok the following month. Meanwhile, Llewelyn was busy on the 'Thomas Shoel' and sent a draft of it to Tavender in February:*

My dear Mr Tavender,

I was very grateful to you for taking my dialect in hand and will surely insert your corrections. It is very good of you to offer to lend me these books on Somerset dialect, but I had better wait until my eyes are stronger and I am more vigorous for I have all I can do at present. I have been very impressed by your kindness in helping me in so many ways and your power of making all information interesting. It has been a pleasure to me to hear from you. Apparently the rumour that Shoel was buried at Norton came from Mr Wilton. I enclose Mr Osbourne's letter for your observation and also your letter from the managing director of the *Western Gazette* who has evidently lost some valuable scraps of information. I have had to have my essay retyped as it stands but I will send you a carbon copy to look over in a week or two, and to question or correct as you think fit.

This weather has been very bad but I am glad to say that I have so far got through it in fair order. I had a very kind letter from Mr Hardin of Bishop's Auckland. I think my essay pleased the family, which was gratifying to me.

I do thank you so much for all your help and understanding. Good Lord! What a villainous motto the Curzon motto is — the Phelips motto even is more friendly! Yours sincerely, Llewelyn Powys. P.S. Thank you for returning the *Atlantic Monthly*. I enclose some letters, but I would like to have them also back, if this is not troubling you too much. P.P.S. Thank you for *British Weekly* just discovered. If I continue to be praised by respectable people I shall think there is something wrong with my soul's health. Thank you very much for letting me see it.

Dear Mr Tavender,

I enclose a MSS draft of my essay on Thomas Shoel. Do you think you could possibly find time to go through it — making any corrections of errors you may notice or suggesting any improvements that come into your head.

I shall be most grateful if you would do this. Was Mitchell's mother Ellen Mitchell? Yours sincerely, Llewelyn Powys. I do hope you will approve of the essay.

Dear Mr Tavender,

I was so grateful for your careful attention and very glad to have these errors put right.

I think you should have been a man of letters rather than quarry owner and glove manufacturer!

I was suspicious of the spelling of 'Grenfell' and I was thinking of writing to Mr Ingilby about it.

I was very pleased to see the photograph of Nancy and will keep it if I may until Dr Goodden returns from Spain. He would be very interested to see it. By an odd coincidence Mr Hardin sent me an account of the old woman's life by the same post. I will send it to you on the chance of it suggesting further notes from you. It is very well written and very sympathetic.

My correspondence with you has been a great pleasure. Yesterday there arrived from Fred Rogers one of Shoel's original published music books with easy anthems and all — a very old looking book costing 5/– and belonging originally to a musician, Henry Johnson — I suppose the father of Bill — who surely had a good bass voice. I am very glad to know that one exists. If you would like to see it I would write and ask whether I could send it to you by registered post. Yours sincerely, Llewelyn Powys. [P.S.] Can you recall any good hearsay about old Mr. Goodden. I would have liked to have written something on him — but he does not seem to have had so much individual character, though a fine representative of his class? Do you remember Wyndham and any of his exploits?

Despite his continued ill-health and the attack of pleurisy that marked the winter of 1935–6, Llewelyn's output of essays at this period was prolific.

It included a series of seasonal articles for The Daily Herald, *a sequence called 'the Poetry of God', completed at the end of 1935, local articles for the* Dorset Echo, *and the first batch of his 'Somerset' series, many of them, like those on Nancy Cooper and the Duke of Monmouth drawing on folk memories of his childhood locality. Llewelyn even got round to penning a piece on Wyndham Goodden's father, vicar of Montacute 1845–85, which because unpromising was never published. In the following letter, Llewelyn sends a draft of 'Nancy Cooper', about the Montacute vagrant, to Tavender for comment. This was later published as 'A Vagabond' in* The Western Gazette, *3 July 1936. Meanwhile 'Thomas Shoel' did the rounds in February to March of 1936 — both as a contribution and for comment. A letter of John Cowper Powys of 12 February tells of its being sent him and his brothers and to T. S.Eliot at* The Criterion. *In the event no-one published it. The third of the following letters speaks of the sudden illness of his brother Bertie. Llewelyn was later to report, in affectionate reminiscence of Bertie, who died in March that year, that his comments on 'Thomas Shoel' were 'regular rude notes' designed to staunch the minutest misrepresentation — see* Letters of John Cowper Powys to His Brother Llewelyn, *II, 211, and* The Letters of Llewelyn Powys, *208.*

Dear Mr Tavender,

Thank you very much for your excellent letter which we greatly enjoyed — Dr Goodden is exactly the same today and insists in driving up to us over the downs and up skiddy tracks where no young man will venture — and yet without any nonsense has a heart of pure gold.

I enclose 'Nancy Cooper'. If you could add to it by any further information I would be glad. I would ever so much like an essay on her to go with the Squire, Parson, Minister, Poet — in my *Somerset Essays* which will be most concerned with Montacute. Yours Llewelyn Powys. [P.S.] This cold wind does me little good. I shall advise you to be careful of it. Your friend, Llewelyn Powys.

My dear Mr Tavender,

Thank you very much for your good letter with enclosures. Your letters are always full of interest and I value them very much. I must thank you for the photographs you sent me. They were very interesting to me and I am glad to possess them, as also were my sisters to see them, especially Miss Katie who always speaks with great affection and appreciation of you. I was very glad to get that Grenville put right and also *Milly* Mitchell, and I am so very proud to possess the photograph of Nancy. It pleases me so much. I have not yet heard about my essay from its second venture, but I have sent a carbon copy to America. I may have difficulty in placing it. My trade is no safe trade. I hear that my *Dorset Essays* which has won me so much applause has not yet sold 1000 copies, so I suppose I shan't get more than £30 in royalties. We live like rats, a gnaw here and a scratch there, but so it should be for it is a wonderful thing to work *at your leisure* and to be independent. Who would not wear the philosopher's short coat in such times? My sisters send you their greetings. We have survived this nipping weather. Yours, my dear friend, Llewelyn Powys.

Dear Mr Tavender,

Indeed I shall be very delighted to receive a rat tail cactus from you — it would be most good of Mrs Tavender, and if you could lend me the article you mention by Mr Grenville I should be very interested and I would also like to see Miss Harlin Bates' lecture. Dr Goodden writes from Spain that he remembers about the Abbey pond but says the water was *shallow*! He instructed the chemist to send me a belladonna plaster and it has done my pleurisy a little good I think. My brother ARP is at the moment very ill which is an anxiety — with a stomach ulcer. This is an anxiety to us.

You are a splendid writer of letters. Your letters are always so full of spirit.

I have been writing an essay on Monmouth. I see that a history of Norton by a Trask says refugees hid in the Montacute woods. This book must be by the old man. I would like to see it and have written to the Rev Harold Trask who is a neighbour. With many thanks for all your care of me. Yours sincerely, Llewelyn Powys.

It is likely in this instance that the Monmouth essay was that published in The Cornhill Magazine *CLIII in June 1936 under the title 'Monmouth: June–July 1685'. Certainly that is the one which was republished in* Somerset Essays. *Another article, adapted from it, was printed first as 'A Royal Failure For Whom Men of Dorset Died' in the* Dorset Daily Echo *on 11 April. March 1936 was a black month for the Powys family, with the death of Bertie on the 15th. Llewelyn was too ill to attend the funeral, Alyse going in his place. Disaster struck on another front too — with the Thomas Shoel essay. Delving into local and family history has its pitfalls, as the following letter displays. Llewelyn's attempts to extricate himself from delicate entanglements were not always subtle, and Tavender's authority and experience saved the day:*

In confidence

My dear Mr Tavender,

For God's sake come to my rescue. I have got into a terrible pickle with Mrs Greenham. Mrs Woodhouse wrote to me telling me she advised me not to put her name into my essay as her *grand* relations of the Glove Factory etc. would not care to see it in the essay. She explained that the poor woman was very eccentric and ragged and subject to be criticised by the clergymen and others — Mr Guppy declaring 'she was an eye-sore' etc. I was indignant and scolded poor Annie Woodhouse for taking so worldly and foolish a point of view — telling her to look at the inside of the pot and not to the outside etc. and the next day sent Mrs Greenham a coat and skirt in very good condition that my wife had just been given by her aunt. This was immediately returned with an abrupt and uncivil note. I then wrote apologising and saying that I myself was without pride of this kind and had sent the clothes in no spirit of patronage etc.

Meanwhile Annie Woodhouse read the selections from my essay, and she resents my reference to his poverty and thinks I have set about deliberately to depreciate him and degrade the Shoel family, and I do not feel as if I can really begin to try to explain matters to anybody so uninformed and so emotional, and I wondered whether you would intervene on my behalf and perhaps divert the firing from Chaldon to Parkstone.

It is possible that your prestige might carry weight, and you might be able to intimidate her by explaining what careful investigations have been made from museums and old records and that far from being abused *I should be praised* for saving Shoel's name from oblivion just in time, and if you possibly can do so make her feel a little sorry for having taken so ignorant and philistine a view and treated me with such extraordinary unfairness. Of course it is all very silly, but also agitating to me, as I would not wish to trouble her and I honour Shoel so much I would not wish to trouble a descendant, but who has ever known a genius who is not poor, except perhaps Voltaire, sly old fox.

For God's sake give your advice and if possible bring peace to these troubled waters. Peace and JUSTICE. I rely upon you, my old friend and good luck to you. Yours Llewelyn Powys. [*In margins*] Could not you say that you and everyone always had heard of his extreme poverty and the poverty is no disgrace to anybody and least of all with poets, and she has completely misjudged the essay, which has been greatly praised, and it is foolish to have pride in material values and disregard intellectual values — but you had better not send the documents to her but say I have investigated at great expense and trouble to myself with no prospect of pecuniary reward but simply out of love and a desire to secure the name of Thomas Shoel a place in English literature — and that my feelings have been very much hurt by her attitude and no one has behaved in such a way before to me in my whole life's experience, and any other talk that might well come from my plenipotentiary! [P.S.] Have you read Charles Trask's book on Norton. It is interesting — I have borrowed it but could lend it. God! What unforeseen snares and pitfalls we get caught in, head over heels! B[ugger]!

Dear Mr Tavender,

What a wise good friend! I think I will not write myself unless she makes another communication — but I am willing to propitiate in any way but not to tamper with the essay which would be invalidated if I tried to make it what she wants — for there is scarcely a single one of Shoel's poems which does not cry out against his poverty and misery brought on by his poverty. I thought it was most valiant of you to come to my rescue at once before I made my appeal and very good of you — for I really was at a lost to know what to do.

I think she must be the proudest woman in Montacute, her pride mounts to 'genius', but I wouldn't for the world hurt her feelings. I thought your story of Cromwell wonderfully appropriate — but my impression is she will never be amenable to reason — for who can hope to get understanding into a head ruled by emotion. It is 'right judgement' that is wanted and this you seem to have in remarkable degree. If she attacks me again I shall get my wife who is herself a writer (and likes always to be addressed as Miss Gregory instead of Mrs Powys) to try to explain. It certainly has been agitating. I think any incident in life where people's feelings are involved cannot be dismissed lightly. Yours, Llewelyn Powys. [P.S.] I was amused by your talk of the harmonium. God bless us all!

The following letter appears to be the last of the batch, and comes with a date of 19 March 1936. It is followed by the draft Obituary which Llewelyn prepared for his friend and correspondent who died suddenly on the 25th of the month. 'Thomas Shoel' was eventually published in Somerset Essays *in 1937, and remains not only one of Llewelyn's most characteristic pieces, but an important source of information on a lost literary figure:*

March 19th 1936

My dear Mr Tavender,

How very good of you to have done all this for me and I think you have a most able mind and a mind with what my father was always praying for — a mind with right judgements. I have put [by] your letter and notes and alterations for the time being until I get the essay accepted and then shall use them all. I enclose this letter from the *Atlantic Monthly*. I am evidently going to have difficulty in placing the essay so perhaps all our agitations will have been meaningless. We will not plan any more about your visit here until the summer is with us. You are hard of hearing and I am without breath but as we have always been able to communicate by the pen we will confine the rewards of meeting to the pleasure of sight and the shake of a hand — though we shall have our interpreters I have little doubt. I cannot find your letter in which you gave the list of the Somerset worthies you wrote of — I have some ten essays lacking for my book, and might try one or two of your gentlemen if I had your list again. I am sending you a copy of my *Dorset Essays* as a March gift. It goes to you with my affection and esteem. Yours sincerely, Llewelyn Powys. [P.S.] I am sorry I was so careless and uninformed about the Mara affair. I will surely see all this is put right. I am as you perhaps know sceptical of all supernatural religion and this attitude is inclined sometimes to lead one into shallow writing.

[OBITUARY]

The death of the old Montacute inhabitant Mr H. G.Tavender at Parkstone, on March 25th at the age of 73 will be a heavy loss to all those of us who liked to learn from him about the old days of Montacute. Mr Tavender at one time was the owner of a stone quarry on Ham Hill and was a capable man of business but his interests were never confined to money making. During the last year it has been my privilege to be in close correspondence with him and I had the greatest respect for his direct, tolerant and understanding mind, a mind which manifested in a remarkable way the deep, solid, unaffected culture that is so often to be found in old Non-conformist circles, where information and learning is sought in all subjects and without any motive in view beyond the pleasure that knowledge itself can give. The Non-conformist culture is solid and liberal and its value in our national life cannot be over-estimated. Even his religious convictions Mr Tavender would never press upon others unduly. Of this I had a very moving example only a week ago. It so happened that I had written of the untimely death of my beloved brother Mr. A. R. Powys, 'he has gone for ever'. Mr Tavender's reply was full of genuine concern over my sorrow and his letter ended in this way, 'Would you perhaps allow me without offence to say that your brother is not necessarily gone for ever.' Llewelyn Powys, Chaldon Herring.

JOHN COWPER POWYS

The Entermores

A Play In Three Acts

THE CHARACTERS

Madeline Entermore	A middle-class lady; the wife of Roland Entermore
Roland Entermore	A poet; the husband of Madeline Entermore
Florian Fay	Editor and joint publisher of 'The Black Pierrot'
Flo Donahue	Barmaid at 'The Goat and Boy'
Theophilus Groteus	Joint publisher, with Florian Fay, of 'The Black Pierrot'
Rev. Bray Smith	Rector of St. Walpurga's church.
Stephen Pontifex	Senior Curate of St. Walpurga's church
Pol Flecker	A street girl
Bess Round	A street girl, the companion of Roland Entermore
Job Swatchy	A ruffian associated with both Pol Flecker and Bess Round
Emma	Mrs Entermore's maid
Sue	A friend and neighbour of Bess Round

ACT ONE

Scene I

The Entermores' Drawing Room.

[*Madeline alone*]

MADELINE My child at any rate shall be brought up in the faith of his fathers. It were horrible to think of an innocent and believing soul like his, so pure and trusting, being denied the consolations of our religion.

[*Enter Roland*]

ROLAND I just came to tell you, Madeline, that I shall not be home to dinner tonight. I am going to meet our friends ...

MADELINE Your friends, you mean!

ROLAND And discuss the new number of the 'L'Outrance' — Florian Fay says —

MADELINE I dislike this paper of yours, Roland.

ROLAND Florian Fay says that if I write a poem of twelve verses he will put it on the first page ...

MADELINE Florian Fay!

ROLAND This number is going to be the most effective of the whole set. O, we're to strike the Philistines a real blow this time.

[*He rubs his hands and walks up and down the room*]

MADELINE I wish you wouldn't use these affected expressions, Roland.

ROLAND What do you mean? Can't you sympathize with me in

anything? You know you promised to let me invest this legacy of ours in the 'Black Pierrot'. You'll be glad enough when our paper begins to pay. Why do you always throw cold water on my schemes?

MADELINE You're talking at random now, Roland. You know very well what I mean. I hate this word 'Philistine'. Is anything honourable? —— it is Philistine. Is anything upright? —— it is Philistine. Is anything simple and pure and direct and virtuous? —— it is Philistine. You are either wilfully suppressing your better self, my friend, or you are lamentably led astray by words.

ROLAND When I say 'Philistine', I mean respectable, commonplace, conventional — everything opposed to the natural play of life.

MADELINE Thank God I am a Philistine, if not to be one means to lose all distinction between right and wrong. Come — let us drop this conversation, Roland, it is distressing to me. It is extremely dangerous for you. You are on the verge of saying things you will regret one day. Let us avoid discussion. You only deceive yourself by these speeches. You know as well as I do that moral laws are necessary for the happiness of all of us — if it was not for what you call conventionality, men would soon be worse than beasts.

ROLAND That is always your way. You command me to stop the conversation and then, when I am forbidden to answer, you shoot your sharpest dart. Yes. Well. Florian is right — women are all the same.

MADELINE Florian, as you call him, knows as much about women as the beetles that breed at the bottom of a pond know about the swallows that skim its surface.

ROLAND Florian is my friend, Madeline — and you may be glad he is. I should have never published my verses at all if it hadn't been for his help and advice.

MADELINE Perhaps it would have been better if you had never published them.

ROLAND What? Not published them? Not published my verses? O, very well, then it is as I always thought. You do not really take any interest in my life. You take ...

MADELINE Too deep an interest in your life, Roland, to care for your present mode of writing. There were poets once ...

ROLAND Enough of this. You have written, I hope, to this Curate of yours to tell him that I refuse to let Tony go to any more of his classes?

MADELINE Roland!

ROLAND Yes, I mean what I say. I have seen something of the influence of these High Church clergymen. I won't have my son taught their dogmas, their tricks and their ridiculous observances.

MADELINE O, it is as I feared. It is as I feared.

[*She throws herself on the sofa and begins to sob*]

ROLAND [*Walking up and down the room in distraction. Aside*] What was it Florian said the other day about women when they cry? Women's tears stamp crueller bonds than Jews' seals. No, I cannot endure this.

[*He bends over her; she still sobs*]

Madeline. Madeline. Don't cry, my darling. Tony shall go where you like and learn what you please —— only don't cry. It is a pity to cry. You don't know how dreadful people look when they cry. There —— that's better. Tony shall go to Mr Pontifex if you wish.

MADELINE Dear Roland! You know you yourself wouldn't wish

our little boy to grow up unloving and disobedient.

ROLAND — Certainly not, dear. [*Aside*] Have these women no trust in Nature?

MADELINE — He will learn to be unselfish — there is no way except by a real living faith to overcome our instincts. And you know you liked Mr Pontifex the other day. He has, you said, no nonsense about him.

ROLAND — [*Aside*] Curates with no nonsense about them are the most dangerous of all. They are like those ginger—beer bottles that people call well 'up' —— you never know when they are going to burst out. [*To Madeline*] Order as you will, my dear. You had most of the trouble in bringing Tony into this world, and it is only fair you should be allowed to introduce him to the next through whatever peep-hole you prefer.

MADELINE — And you won't go tonight to see those people, Roland? Stay tonight with me. I do so miss you when you are away. I seem to see so little of you now.

ROLAND — [*Patting her head*] Poor child —— I am afraid I must go all the same. You see, I promised.

MADELINE — Do you know what I think Hell is paved with?

ROLAND — No?

MADELINE — Promises that are kept too well.

Scene 2

Inside the 'Goat and Boy'

FLORIAN — Well, Flo? What kind of a temper are you in today?

FLO — None the better for seeing you, Mr Fay.

FLORIAN How red you are, Flo! Somebody has been saying something to make you blush.

FLO Well, it wasn't you, at any rate.

FLORIAN I never say rude things.

FLO Nor do them either, I suppose?

FLORIAN Is kissing rude?

FLO [*Very red*] Don't blarney me now. You don't think I'm going to let you kiss me again, do you, Mr Fay?

FLORIAN You barmaids must have very dull lives.

FLO Not so dull as you imagine, Mr Fay.

FLORIAN What has become of the violets I gave you yesterday, Flo?

FLO They died. Do you think violets last more than a day in London?

[*Enter Theophilus*]

FLORIAN I suppose not — O, here is Groteus. I must have a little talk with him. Two glasses of special Scotch please. Well, Theo, how are you?

THEOPHILUS I am in one of my nervous moods today. It is dreadful bad my nerves are. Everything I look at seems on the point of sticking knives into me. I really feel as if I have absolutely no skin.

FLORIAN How interesting you would look without any skin, Theophilus. You would look like a portrait of Marsyas.

THEOPHILUS Yes, but the world is more cruel than Apollo, Florian.

FLORIAN We are indeed less fortunate than the ancients. They lived while they lived and when they could live no longer somebody killed them or they killed themselves. We cease living but continue to exist.

THEOPHILUS O, remind me not of my existence. I am weary, so thoroughly sick of it. I had almost arrived at the secret of the true detachment when you spoke. I had almost become somebody else. I had begun to be you.

FLORIAN [*Starts*] For Heaven's sake, my dear boy, don't speak of anything so commonplace. Altruism is the most odious of truisms. It always makes me think of Mr Herbert Spencer and afternoon tea.

THEOPHILUS But it is very much in the air just now.

FLORIAN In the air, indeed! Yes, it is in the air. I only hope it will remain there and not come any nearer.

THEOPHILUS Society is indeed degenerate.

FLORIAN O, name it not!

THEOPHILUS In the old days people tried to be witty: now they talk Socialism.

FLORIAN That is being witty. Have you read Mr Shaw's new play?

THEOPHILUS Mr Shaw, who is he?

FLORIAN A melodramatic writer of the time. They tell me he imitates Charles Dickens — brings in servants and shop assistants and manufacturers and young girls.

THEOPHILUS O, stop, my dear friend.

FLORIAN Yes, it is distressing to think of. He belongs to the class of Inspired Harlequins.

THEOPHILUS Harlequin?

FLORIAN Yes — the people who compel the British public to laugh by revolving in a surprising series of scandalous rotations.

THEOPHILUS Revolving?

FLORIAN Yes. Like a top. You never can tell which side they will come up.

THEOPHILUS It all sounds extremely uncomfortable. Did you say clever?

FLORIAN Well, no, not as one would say clever. The Public, my dear friend, the Public creates this sort of thing.

THEOPHILUS Yes, I suppose it does.

FLORIAN Creates it by its own excessive stupidity. It is so stupid that it turns into brilliant wit everything that is said in its presence. It is the old story of a dark night and a jumping cracker. Ladies shrink and tighten their petticoats but they really enjoy it.

THEOPHILUS: What do they not enjoy?

FLORIAN What indeed?

THEOPHILUS The decline of wit in these days is really deplorable.

FLORIAN The English Public puts its real geniuses into prison.

THEOPHILUS It does — it does. I can hardly pass a policeman myself without a shudder.

FLORIAN Genius consists in re-selecting the materials of the universe. When this is done in practice the elements that are left out rebel.

THEOPHILUS And of course they have the Old Original Artificer on their side. O dear, Providence is dreadfully like the President of the Royal Society of British Architects.

FLORIAN Well, my friend, when are you going to let me have that short story for 'L'Outrance'?

THEOPHILUS I haven't begun it yet. By the way, is all this true about Roland's legacy?

FLORIAN Yes, he has — or rather his wife has — a large mass of money. I am going to invest it in our dear 'Black Pierrot'.

THEOPHILUS Mrs Entermore will have something to say about that.

FLORIAN Roland will be here soon. I think he carries poems in his shoes, he always comes well supplied.

THEOPHILUS You shall have that story tomorrow afternoon, Florian.

FLORIAN Shall I? O, here he is. How do you do, Paul Verlaine.

[*Enter Roland*]

ROLAND How are you, Florian? Ah, Theophilus — glad to see you. Good evening, Flo! A plain Peppermint, please! What do you mean by calling me Paul Verlaine, Florian?

FLORIAN Because you are less like him than anyone I know and there must be affinity between opposites. Well — have you brought your poem? Ah! I see. Thanks — ah! 'Thunder'— yes, we must read it at once. [*Putting it into his pocket*] Well, how are your domestic affairs?

ROLAND I have agreed to let Tony go to Mr Pontifex.

FLORIAN You could not act more wisely.

THEOPHILUS Wisely?

FLORIAN Yes. The only sensible system of education nowadays is to teach children what you know to be untrue.

ROLAND You rely upon reaction?

FLORIAN I rely upon nothing — but I know children.

ROLAND It is a triumph for my wife.

FLORIAN Indulge her in that delusion.

ROLAND Women are very clever.

FLORIAN [*Looking round*] Enough of that, dear Roland — there is nobody listening to us now — let us put aside that old-fashioned mask and speak the truth.

ROLAND The truth?

FLORIAN Don't pretend to misunderstand me — of course we always call them clever. In novels we even use the word 'subtle' — but we know — well — we know...

ROLAND What do we know?

FLORIAN That they are really angelically and exquisitely stupid — far more stupid than children.

THEOPHILUS That is correctly said. I have seldom found a woman who didn't think she understood me — and I have never found a child who didn't.

FLORIAN They imagine our vices are drink and — and other women.

THEOPHILUS Ha! Ha! Ha!

ROLAND Whereas?

FLORIAN This affair between France and Germany looks serious.The French have their hands full just now. Well, the concordat's gone.

ROLAND The free-thinkers are persecuting the Church with some fanaticism, aren't they, Florian?

FLORIAN It is folly. Such a nation of artists ought to know that the art of life requires as much superstition as can be found.

THEOPHILUS You mean in others.

FLORIAN Certainly. I hate this Utopian Tea Party sort of Universal Toleration.

ROLAND — But surely, my dear Florian, Catholicism is either true or it is false. I don't want persecution, but I think the time has come for all this nonsense to be swept away.

FLORIAN — Roland! Roland! When will you stop using those silly words 'true' and 'false'? Things are either agreeable or disagreeable. I think Catholicism is agreeable — I like to see it — I like to know it is there.

ROLAND — But these priests! These clergymen!

FLORIAN — A wise man can find his account even in them. Somebody must be left, I suppose, to amuse the women.

THEOPHILUS — If it was only the priests ...

FLORIAN — I know what you are thinking of, only your nerves won't allow you to speak.

THEOPHILUS — [*Sighing*] Yes, it is certainly strange how the word 'God' upsets me. I never feel quite myself after hearing it — even in an A.B.C.

ROLAND — I am afraid I must be going now.

FLORIAN — Why, you have only just come.

ROLAND — Yes, but I was later than I expected. I had an engagement on the way.

FLORIAN — You still confine yourself to talking on these occasions? During these engagements?

ROLAND — What d'you mean?

FLORIAN — O, you mustn't be angry. Of course we know all about your little parties at the Albany.

ROLAND — Well, what if you do? Am I to live perpetually in an atmosphere of damned propriety? Am I to see nothing but clergymen? Am I to hear nothing but sermons? Am I never to meet one human being who appears what he is — who says what he really feels. Is my cup of pleasure always to be blocked with conventional ice? O, it is wretched — wretched! When I consider how short life is and how certain death is and how sure we are that there is nothing after death — I say it is cruel to be hemmed in and restricted, balked and baffled, fettered by a thousand invisible chains like this. Besides, you have no idea how nice, yes, how nice, Florian, these so-called unfortunate women really are.

FLORIAN I think we can imagine, Theo, eh?

THEOPHILUS I shiver to think of it. Ostrich feathers and barrels of cognac.

ROLAND O, you may smile and jeer, Florian — you may smile and jeer. I know what you are thinking. I know the heartless way you regard all these things. But I tell you — between my wife's conventionality and your cynicism I sometimes feel I should go mad. But I will not go mad. I will live out my own life. I must and will have realities — [*He stamps his foot*] — Realities! Realities! Realities!

THEOPHILUS A scene! It has actually become a scene. How extremely uncomfortable.

FLORIAN You need not get so excited. I suppose you did not come here tonight to tell us this.

ROLAND No, you didn't expect this, did you? You expected me to bring you poems — pretty, decadent, immoral poems for your cursed 'Black Pierrot'. Poems! I tell you, Florian, when I see all the misery that there is in London, when I talk to these unfortunate women and hear about their wretched lives, I feel -- I feel as though I couldn't write another poem.

[*Exit Roland*]

THEOPHILUS We shan't be financed, Florian — the 'Black Pierrot' will be exploded.

FLORIAN And women at the bottom of it again! It is too vexing. Just as he was going to come down with a thousand pounds. And we should have had such a lovely cover next quarter. Montmorency had promised it a blue hamadryad on a yellow ground. O dear — so, after all, the British Public must go unconverted. And women at the bottom of it again!

Scene 3

The Vicarage of the Rev. Bray Smith.

[*Enter Rev. Bray Smith and Pontifex*]

BRAY SMITH O, I am so glad to see you, Pontifex. Sit down. I wanted to talk to you about the Entermores. Have a cigarette. You will find them under that New Testament. They are the old kind — Players Medium Navy Cut, you know, not too expensive. That's right. No thanks — O, well, perhaps just one, since we are in the way of being dissipated.

PONTIFEX This feels quite naughty, vicar. It wouldn't do for Mrs Heliobottom to see us now — would it? O, a dreadful woman! She buttonholed me yesterday ...

BRAY SMITH [*Anxiously*] I hope, my dear Pontifex, you were discreet.

PONTIFEX O, don't fear me. There are limits to my diplomacy of course, but I think Heliobottom will not be the one to discover them. By the way, the off. at early ceb. this morning was only thirty pounds.

BRAY SMITH No more? I hope that unfortunate mistake you made the other day, Pontifex, when you put on the red stole instead of the violet, has had nothing to do with this.

PONTIFEX O, nothing, nothing. What a wonderful victory that was on Saturday of Wales over the All Blacks. I should like to have seen it. By the way, Tom Turner has joined my Boy's Club. I think he will do quite well now his sister has gone to service. An excellent stroke of yours, Vicar, getting that girl out of the way.

BRAY SMITH [*Complacently*] Yes, she was a danger — a danger — I do care in these cases. And now, Pontifex, about these Entermores. You and Mrs Entermore are, I understand ...

PONTIFEX One thing first, Vicar, while I think of it. Our friends the Protestants are making themselves troublesome again. I hear they propose coming to break up our evensong tomorrow.

BRAY SMITH [*Startled*] You don't say so!

PONTIFEX I heard one fellow — you know him — the coal-heaver in Paradise St. — Bob Flontem — swears he would revenge Mr Kensit's death on you.

BRAY SMITH [*Moving nervously*] On me!

PONTIFEX O, he only mentioned you as being the most prominent English Catholic of this neighbourhood — but he is a rash and violent man — they say he usually carries a large piece of iron about with him.

BRAY SMITH A piece of iron.

PONTIFEX Yes. Is it not a curious idea?

BRAY SMITH I don't see that it is so curious. Outrageous, I call it. [*After a pause*] Well, as I was saying, Pontifex, Mrs Entermore ...

PONTIFEX [*In a thick voice*] Do you know anything of a paper called 'The Clarion'?

BRAY SMITH No. What's that got to do with Mrs Entermore?

PONTIFEX I see it now and then in her drawing-room. It is anti-Christian, you know — but I think we ought to read all sides.

BRAY SMITH Its influence must be extremely pernicious.

PONTIFEX Blatchford is a good fellow.

BRAY SMITH Blatchford?

PONTIFEX He is the editor, you know. He imagines he is fighting against Christianity — and I suppose he has seen nothing of it except for a crazy evangelical or two — or a strong broad churchman. I should like to have a talk with him. I cannot help think that if he met with real Catholic doctrines...

BRAY SMITH You wouldn't do any good. These infidels are hopelessly narrow-minded.

PONTIFEX But what has what you call his counter-blasts to do with an extreme Socialist?

BRAY SMITH Ah, I thought you would come to that soon. That accounts for your interest in him. Pontifex, these Socialist tendencies of yours will lead you into trouble one day.

PONTIFEX If we could only work Socialism on Christian lines, Vicar, all would be well. Christian Socialism …

BRAY SMITH By 'Christian' of course you mean 'Catholic', Pontifex.

PONTIFEX What else? Christian Socialism does not aim at destroying private property. It does not interfere with the existing order of Church and State. It does not encourage the lower orders to isolate themselves or engage in class war. It does not ...

BRAY SMITH [*Interrupting*] O, all right, Pontifex, you needn't go on. I understand — and now let us come to the matter about which I really wanted to see you. Mrs Entermore is a close friend of yours.

PONTIFEX I hope you have not been listening to any absurd gossip.

BRAY SMITH If I did, Pontifex — if I did — the priests of St Walpurga's must not be in the mouth of anyone.

PONTIFEX [*Helping himself to a cigarette*] Well, Rector?

BRAY SMITH You and Mrs Entermore have been intimate for many weeks. Her child, she tells me, is to come to you every morning. Well, er, er, I hear — of course this is confidential, Pontifex — I hear that the Entermores have suddenly become rich — an uncle in Australia or something of that sort has left them a large sum of money. Well — I thought — in fact, er, it seemed to me — suitable and — er, adequate, you know, that some of this money should go to help building the new Church in Wrench St. I am tired of collections, they bring in so little — and of course I cannot — it would not be fair to Mrs Bray Smith and Louise — bear the expense myself. So you see what I am aiming at, Pontifex! Ha! Ha! Ha! We're quite Machiavellian, aren't we? Well, it's the wisdom of the serpent applied to — to — applied to the erection of a dovecot for doves — eh? Ha!

PONTIFEX [*Eyeing him with disgust*] And if I refuse this little commission?

BRAY SMITH [*With a cunning look*] Then, Pontifex, I shall be compelled to take some sort of notice of what these gossips say.

PONTIFEX — [*Rising*] This is really outrageous, sir. Am I to be made a tool to extract money from...

BRAY SMITH — Calm yourself, my friend, calm yourself and look at this matter quietly. The situation is indeed quite clear. I, the Rector of St. Walpurga's, hear constant rumours that my Senior Curate is on terms of, well, we'll say on too intimate terms with a wealthy lady of my parish — these rumours may be false.

PONTIFEX — May!

BRAY SMITH — Don't interrupt me. These rumours, I repeat, may be false. Personally, of course, I am sure they are false — but how can they be publicly refuted? They can be publicly refuted by definite evidence that this friendship of yours for Mrs Entermore results in a blessing for our good Mother, the Church. Do you see now? Let the lady make a large subscription — say, twenty thousand pounds or so — and all evil tongues will be hushed in admiration for her goodness.

PONTIFEX — I flatly decline to have anything to do with this detestable scheme. Dismiss me if you please — I dismiss you! It is just such worldly, plotting, sly toads as you that bring the name of Priest into odour and shame with honourable people.

[*He goes towards the door*]

BRAY SMITH — One minute, Pontifex. Before we separate, I might add that, if you had seen your way to helping your Mother the Church in this matter, instead of pouring vulgar abuse on me, Providence would probably have rewarded you by giving you many opportunities of intercourse with your friend. I should have probably selected as architect your brother.

PONTIFEX — My brother!

BRAY SMITH And of course all architectural details — windows, screens, reredos and that sort of thing — would have been left to you and the donor of the generous gift to decide upon in combination. You would, in fact — as is only due to your well-known artistic taste — have represented myself in the matter.

PONTIFEX [*Obviously relaxing but concealing his weakness under a new outburst*] I will not be fooled in this way. Let me tell you, once and for all, I will not. I know you and I am the only person in this parish who knows you — Good morning!

[*Exit*]

BRAY SMITH There he goes — silly, silly boy! He thinks me a hypocrite. I could see it — a hypocrite and a scoundrel. And yet all I want is to squeeze a little money out of a pretty woman's purse, while he would squeeze the blood out of her body if he could. And I shouldn't be surprised if he hadn't already done it. O, these idealists, these idealists!

Scene 4

Outside the 'Goat and Boy'

POL 'As that bloke given you any more 'oof?

BESS If he 'as, 'taint your affair. 'es a reglar toff — none of yer arf and arfs.

POL Is 'ee a soft — is 'ee going to pay yer to keep off the game?

BESS 'Ee's a real gentleman.

POL Ho! Ho! Ho! So, it's come to that, has it!

BESS [*Turning her head*] I don't want any of your lip.

POL — [*Hesitating*] You ain't a goin' to take Jobie away from me agen, are you? I tell yer, if you do I shall kill someone, so look out.

BESS — What do I want with Jobie? Keep your Jobie.

POL — Don't insult my boy.

BESS — A bletherin', boozin', bloomin' bounder.

POL — Is 'ee? I know who's dyin' to 'ave 'im, all the same — an' who isn't goin' to 'ave 'im. Ta-ta! Lady Warmit!

[*Exit Pol. Roland appears*]

ROLAND — O, I am so glad to see you, Bess. I have been to Regent Street, to Piccadilly — I have been everywhere looking for you.

BESS — Don't squeeze me so, you wicked boy. [*He kisses her*] Now! Naughty ...

ROLAND — There's no harm in kissing, I suppose?

BESS — Wot if yer wife saw us now ?

ROLAND — [*With a perceptible tremble*] O, my wife goes her own way and I go mine.

BESS — I say, old boy — I 'aven't 'ad so much as a drop of Scotch today.

ROLAND — Shall we go in here?

BESS — [*Indifferently*] As you like. There's a 'lectric organ at Bardolph's ...

ROLAND — But Bardolph's is so far away.

BESS — Three stations by the tube and a 'alfpenny bus — we'd be there while we're talkin' about it.

ROLAND — I'd sooner go in here. They know me — they let us have a private room. I want to have a nice long conversation with you.

BESS — All right, please yourself. I'm sure I don't want to inconvenience you.

ROLAND — But still ... [*Aside*] I certainly don't want to encounter Florian. [*To Bess*] If you like ...

BESS — [*Fretfully*] For Lord's sake, come in somewhere, do — I'm gettin' cold. [*As they go in*] I say, Kiddie, you'll let me have a few shillings tonight, won't you? I can't ask you if there are a lot of people inside.

ROLAND — We'll see about that when we say goodbye.

[*They enter*]

Scene 5

Inside the 'Goat and Boy'.

FLO — Now, you shut up, Mr Fay. You ought to be ashamed of yourself saying things like that — oughtn't he, Mr Groteus?

FLORIAN — Nonsense, Flo. Give me another Benedictine and don't talk nonsense. I believe we shall get the 'Black Pierrot' through, after all. I saw Roland the next day and he was in one of his apologetic moods — was sorry he had called us cynics — he had begun to think we were quite right about women. He said he thought this paper would do a great deal of good.

THEOPHILUS — Did he say 'good'?

FLORIAN — Well, he didn't exactly say that — I shouldn't have let him say that. There we are certainly rather shaky, metaphysically speaking, and we must not be dogmatic.

THEOPHILUS I have never liked the sound of the word 'good'. There is a heavy vibration about it, isn't there?

FLORIAN I suppose it has to be like that as a contrast, you know.

THEOPHILUS You must have accepted a great number of Roland's poems.

FLORIAN No — only three — I escaped with three.

THEOPHILUS They are quite hopeless, of course.

FLORIAN O, absolutely. The old nonsense. That absurd invention, the Living God, hovering about as usual interviewing fallen women.

THEOPHILUS This is a new aspect of our friend, this fondness of his for Piccadilly girls.

FLORIAN [*With a theatrical gesture, striding across the room*] Yes, it is an obstacle in my path which I must o'erleap or perish — the fate of the 'Black Pierrot' hangs in the balance. Our fate, my dear Theophilos, hangs in the balance; for, to confess candidly, we live upon fools, like the rest.

THEOPHILUS [*Meditatively*] You would be in a hole if the 'Black Pierrot' came to an end.

FLORIAN We.

THEOPHILUS You — I have a private income.

FLORIAN Ah — your aunt! Yes, I forgot your aunt! That is certainly a very private income, Theo.

THEOPHILUS But you think there is danger of these ostrich feathers getting before us with Roland's money?

FLORIAN [*Thoughtfully*] They have a genius for exciting pity. They trade more upon the pity of the weak than upon the passion of the strong. A silly romantic fool like

Roland is a very God-send to them. They will get money out of him on the excuse that they want to give up their profession.

THEOPHILUS Will they give it up?

FLORIAN [*Raising his eyebrows with a gesture of weary indifference*] Perhaps.

[*Enter Roland Entermore & Bess. Entermore carrying two glasses*]

ROLAND [*Speaking to Flo*] We will drink these in here. Come on, my child, I have got your glass.

[*Sees Florian and Theophilus. They both rise*]

O — ah — I did not expect to meet you here. These are friends of mine, Bess — Mr Fay and Mr Groteus.

BESS 'Ope you're all well. Me and Roland just 'appened to drop in, 'aving nothing better to do. [*Drinks*] 'Ere's luck.

FLORIAN We are very glad to see you, Roland.

THEOPHILUS Yes — you interrupted a distressing conversation.

ROLAND [*In a low voice to Florian*] I thought I'd give the poor girl a drink. She seemed cold and wretched out there. I just happened to meet her.

BESS [*To Theophilus*] That was a dreadful murder in Shoreditch this morning. I 'ope they catch that fellow. It is a wonder to me 'ow these murderers can go about and look like other people.

THEOPHILUS [*Shuddering visibly and echoing her words*] — like other people.

BESS They must 'ave bloodstains in their souls if they 'aven't on their 'ands. And these respectable people, too, wot live by blackmailing! But I tell you who I think are worse than the whole lot — those able-bodied fellows wot live on the misery of poor women and girls. Them — I always say God'll let off the poor devils as couldn't 'elp it, and send these rich ones as could 'elp it packing to 'ell.

THEOPHILUS [*Shuddering*] Very true, very true. [*Moving his chair away from her and going to sit by Florian*] Well, Roland, and how are your domestic affairs?

ROLAND [*Frowns at him*] O, you mean my housekeeper and boot-boy?

THEOPHILUS Your housekeeper!

BESS Don't mind me, gentlemen — I know very well that none of you tells me what your real name is, or whether you are married or single. [*To Roland, drawing from her pocket a paper, in a loud whisper*] Look here, to show you I 'aven't told you a lie — 'ere's the receipt of those boots wot you give me the money for. You can see them, I've got them on, and the stockings, too. [*She pulls up her dress and shows the boots and stockings*]

FLORIAN [*Aside to Theophilus*] Did you hear that? He's begun making a fool of himself.

THEOPHILUS Probably this is one of many.

ROLAND [*Putting his hand round her ankle*] Poor little wench — you are thin as a rake.

BESS [*Pulling down her skirts*] Now then, none of that — I say, Kiddie, may I have another Scotch? I'll pay for it with my own money. [*She takes out her purse*]

ROLAND Nonsense. [*He gets up and goes to the bar and returns*] Won't you fellows drink something?

FLORIAN No thank you, Roland. By the way, I have secured a splendid article for the 'Black Pierrot' from Professor Fïchslabin. He smashes up once for all this delusion of the spiritual world.

BESS I believe in God, but I don't know anything about the other one.

FLORIAN What other one?

THEOPHILUS Never mind that.

BESS Him wot they call Jesus. They say he 'adn't no father. Well, I 'ave seen Little Titch and The Fat Boy of Hampstead — they're freaks — but a man with no father! Do you believe in it, Mr Fay?

FLORIAN Ah, Theo ...

BESS I've known wot 'tis to be starving for a day and a night and I've known wot it is to be took to prison and when I was starvin' I said, 'O, God, send someone along,' and he did, and when I was in prison I said, 'O, God, get me out of here,' and he did.

FLORIAN Singular coincidence, Theo.

THEOPHILUS Hush. Damned lies.

ROLAND How curious to think that you have actually known what it is to be in prison.

BESS Very horrid, I think — and [*reproachfully*] if I go on as I am going now, I shall probably be in prison again.

FLORIAN [*Aside to Theophilus*] Do you mark that? She is beginning — I know that tone. O, she's safe for a pension. Did you mark that?

THEOPHILUS Very well, Florian. Fool her, draw her, she's a bit in drink — she may disgust him.

FLORIAN [*Meditatively*] It is an extraordinary place, prison.

BESS What do you know about it?

FLORIANFLORIAN O, one hears things now and then.

BESS It's a horrible place, I can tell you — they have no feeling for anybody in those places. I was in for fourteen shillings. They came to me the next morning and said, 'Come on out, you, your fine's been paid.' 'But I have not a friend in the world,' cried I. 'It must be a mistake.' 'Out with you, and don't waste our time,' they said. When I was outside, who do you think I found waiting for me?

ROLAND Who?

FLORIAN Lord Faust?

THEOPHILUS The Marquis of Carabas?

BESS Moll Flanagan — an old drunk girl, who's drinking herself to death. I had given her a drink the day before — afterwards she picked up with someone and was lucky that night — she saw me with the cop and, next morning, she came and paid my fine.

ROLAND That's what I call real nobility. I hope you thanked her, Bess. God reward her!

BESS She cried a lot when she saw me and said she was an Irishwoman — and we went off an' 'ad a Scotch.

ROLAND Well, that's a story that reconciles you to human nature. So all she said was 'I'm an Irishwoman' when you came out?

BESS She put her arms round me and hugged me and she cried a lot.

FLORIAN [*Aside to Theophilus*] That's done it. He's good for thirty shillings a week now.

THEOPHILUS Forty — forty!

BESS — [*To Roland*] I must go now, dear. It doesn't look well if I come home late. These landladies are so suspicious, they ask all sorts of questions. [*Aside to him*] Come out and say goodbye, Kiddie.

ROLAND — Excuse me a moment, you fellows. I will be back in a minute.

[*Exit Roland and Bess*]

FLORIAN — [*Walking*] Now she'll have him — a five pound note to a farthing she'll have him now.

THEOPHILUS — Your expressions have become vulgar, my friend.

FLORIAN — [*Stamping his foot*] It is too annoying! We want every penny he's got for the 'Black Pierrot'. To be defeated by these women! Damn them! I say, damn them!

THEOPHILUS — But, after all, what are a few five pound notes out of his thousands?

FLORIAN — It is not a matter of a few. I tell you, I know this Entermore — when once he has got an idea into his head, a cart and six horses could not get it out. I tell you, the thing won't end with this girl. Why should it? I tell you, I know these Romantic fools. We shall have soon a scheme for reforming all the whores in London.

THEOPHILUS — You display a good deal of emotion, my friend.

FLORIAN — O, of course, I don't really care — The 'Black Pierrot' can go to smash, if it will. I shall have the time to write.

THEOPHILUS — I didn't know you wrote anything except circulars and prospectuses.

FLORIAN — You are insulting, Theo.

THEOPHILUS — You are ridiculous, Florian.

[*Re-enter Roland*]

ROLAND [*Sitting down on the bench with a meditative air*] What a strange world this is!

FLORIAN [*Aside*] That is how they always begin, these fools, when they are about to confess something especially idiotic.

ROLAND The world is very hard upon these poor girls.

FLORIAN Eh? What?

ROLAND Such as this Bess.

FLORIAN O, don't be anxious about her. She is in the amorous arms of Lord Don Juan by this time.

ROLAND Never again, Florian! Never again! [*Rising*] This girl of mine has given up that sort of life for good and all. I am going to look out for respectable rooms for her.

THEOPHILUS I would leave her where she is, if I were you.

ROLAND Where she is?

THEOPHILUS I mean in her present lodging. I fancy she speaks the truth when she says her landlady is a shrew. If you get her these new rooms, she will be able to take anyone she likes there.

ROLAND [*Drily*] I see you think I am being made a fool of.

FLORIAN You are generous, you are generous.

ROLAND The truth is neither of you fellows has the least idea of the inherent goodness of human nature.

THEOPHILUS *Miserere nobis*!

FLORIAN That is not a very orthodox doctrine, is it?

ROLAND I don't care what it is. It is what I feel. In cases such as this, implicit and absolute trust is the only thing that pays.

FLORIAN Come, Theo, it is time for us to go. [*Sneering*] I hope your beautiful trust will be justified.

THEOPHILUS [*Leering*] It won't, if I can help it.

[*They exit*]

ROLAND [*Solemnly*] I have made myself responsible for this girl, and may God confound me if ever I desert her.

SCENE 6

Outside the 'Goat and Boy'

[*Enter Bess*]

BESS Of course, 'ee can't expect me to live on forty shillings a week like a common workman. I must 'ave wot I'm used to. 'Ee's a nice gentleman. Heigho — I feel despondent tonight. I wish one of the boys would come along.

[*Enter Jobie*]

JOBIE 'Allo, Bess, old girl. Come an' 'ave a drink.

BESS Where's your new wife, Jobie?

JOBIE Pol? O, she's no good — she 'ides 'er money. Yes, that's the truth, Gawd 'elp me — she 'ides 'er money.

BESS [*Gently*] Say, Jobie, you come 'ome with me. Never mind Pol. Look wot I've got. [*She shows him money*]

JOBIE [*Hesitating*] You're no grass, Bess — you're a girl wot 'asn't got no cheek. I like a girl wot can make a fellow laugh.

BESS [*Reproachfully*] I love yer better than Pol, Jobie — and look here — I've got a bloke now — a real gentleman wot is payin' me every week.

JOBIE O, yer 'ave, 'ave you?

BESS Yes. An' you shall drink all 'ee gives me — every penny of it, Jobie. Come, Jobie. Come, Jobie, dear.

JOBIE Well, I'll be blowed!

[*Exit Bess and Jobie together*]

ACT TWO

SCENE I

Inside the 'Goat and Boy'.

[*Theophilus and Pol*]

THEOPHILUS [*Putting his arm around her*] Well, Polly, dear, when are we going to have some nice little evening together again as we used to have?

POL [*Sulkily*] Yes — a lot of nice little evenings I've 'ad since I first knew you.

THEOPHILUS You don't regret anything, I hope?

POL [*Bitterly*] O, no — I don't regret anything — if I did there might be some relief.

THEOPHILUS Well — you have chosen your own bed and you must lie on it.

POL [*Rejecting his hand*] 'Tisn't for you to say that to me.

THEOPHILUS O, all right — if you choose to be ungrateful you can. But after all I've done for you...

POL [*With flashing eyes, standing up*] Done for me! Yes, that is what you call it — you men — you cowards! You get your pleasure out of us and you get everything, then, because you do not throw us at once into the river, you pride yourselves on your kindness — you men, you cowards! You dole out your miserable pittance to us and we have to lie, lie, lie, lie to get enough drink to make us forget.

THEOPHILUS [*Going*] O, if you are in that mood I have nothing more to say to you. You'd better stay where you are.

POL — [*Sinking down on a chair and sobbing*] Stop, Theo, I didn't mean it, Theo.

THEOPHILUS — That's right — now you're a sensible girl again — that's right. Now you are pretty little Polly again.

[*She shudders*]

POL — What do you want me to do, Theo?

THEOPHILUS — Something quite simple. You must go to Roland Entermore's house — you must see his wife and you must tell her that Bess Round and Job Swatchy are on her husband's money. You can say that both you and Bess have received money from Roland and that he has been ...

POL — I ain't goin' to bring Roland Entermore into trouble for you, Theo — you know well enough 'ee 'as never given us anything 'cept wot anybody can give a girl. I believe — yes, I believe he's the only good man in London.

THEOPHILUS — You will do just what I say, Pol. What! Are you going to let Bess Round carry off your young man and not do anything?

POL — Curse Bess! I've not spoken to her for days.

THEOPHILUS — And such a nice young man, too. So quiet! So sober!

POL — Enuff about 'im, Theo. 'Ee's no worse than you. [*She remains thoughtful for some while*] Curse her! Curse her! Curse her!

THEOPHILUS — It's no good cursing her if you don't do anything. I expect she's laughing at you now with Jobie. [*Slowly watching the influence of his words*] I think I can hear her laughing. Listen! You can about hear them speak: 'Well, old Pol, I guess, is a bit down in her luck about us' — that's what they're saying. Fleerin' over you,

Pol, old girl — fleerin' over you.

POL — I'll do what you tell me, Theo. If Roland stops giving Bess money, I believe Jobie will come back to me.

THEOPHILUS — Of course he will, my lass, of course he will.

POL — Well, I'll do what you tell me.

THEOPHILUS — That's right. Give me a kiss. [*Kisses her*] Come out for a moment and I'll explain everything. [*Aside*] This will undermine Mr Roland's philanthropy a little. Now for Flo ...

Scene 2

Inside the 'Goat and Boy'

[*Theophilus and Flo*]

THEOPHILUS — Now then, Flo — do you want to do a kindness to myself and Florian?

FLO — I would do next to anything for Mr Florian, but next to nothing for you, you ugly Cycliban.

THEOPHILUS — Well, Mr Florian wanted to ask you himself — but he was afraid.

FLO — Afraid!

THEOPHILUS — Yes, afraid of hurting your moral feelings.

FLO — O, it's something shady, is it?

THEOPHILUS — Florian could never ask you himself but it would be doing him a very good turn.

FLO — Well, out with it Mephistopheles — and don't stand there leerin' and nodding.

THEOPHILUS — He wants you to go and call upon Mrs Entermore.

FLO — Mrs Entermore!

THEOPHILUS — Yes. And tell her about her husband's bringing girls in here and that sort of thing.

FLO — For shame, Mr Groteus!

THEOPHILUS — Well – don't you like my proposal? What's wrong with it?

FLO — Give away a 'usband to 'is wife? I have some 'onour, Mr Groteus.

THEOPHILUS — He ought to have been faithful to her. It's his own fault.

FLO — An' wot's she done? That's wot I asks. She 'ooked 'im first of all. Depend on it, 'ee was sorry when 'ee was married. A man who's faithful to a shrew wot 'ooked 'im into marriage, ain't anything less than a shrew.

THEOPHILUS — Then you have no principles, Mrs Turnover.

FLO — I ain't. It's 'ard not to pity these poor blokes wot wakes to find 'esselves married.

THEOPHILUS — But he has deceived her – deceived her abominably.

FLO — Deceivin' be blowed! Is it deceivin' to breathe? Is it deceivin' to eat and drink? Is it deceivin' to walk in the air?

THEOPHILUS — You are talking nonsense.

FLO — Well then, it's deceivin' to make love to a pretty girl, for that's as natural as breathin' and walkin'.

THEOPHILUS — You are immoral, Mrs Turnover.

FLO — You are the devil, Mr Stoat.

THEOPHILUS — But you'll do it all the same, won't you, Flo? You'll put on your best hat and you'll go and just call upon the lady. Ladies like Mrs Entermore think that people in your position, Flo, don't know how to dress properly or how to behave properly.

FLO Curse their eyes, don't they? I'll show them.

THEOPHILUS And Mr Florian wished me to beg you to accept this — [*Offers five pound note*] — to buy yourself proper clothes to go in.

FLO [*Taking it and holding it at arm's length, hesitantly*] And yet I don't like it. It seems a sort of blood money.

THEOPHILUS O, I see you're afraid to call upon a real lady. You think she'll put you out of the house.

FLO I'm not afraid of anyone. I'm as good as any of them.

THEOPHILUS Well — you'll go then? It's only a call. You'll get into conversation and you'll talk about Roland's coming here and the girls he brings here.

FLO I shan't do anything of the kind.

THEOPHILUS No — no — of course. [*Pushing her out*] You won't, of course you won't. What sort of hat will suit you best, I wonder, Flo?

FLO Well — I warn you, Mr Theo, I shan't say anything dishonourable.

THEOPHILUS No — no, no, of course you won't. You'll probably meet some swell in that drawing-room who'll want to mash you, Flo.

FLO Well, understand, Mr Stoat — Theo — I won't do anything dishonourable

[*He pushes her out*]

Scene 3

Mrs Entermore's drawing room.

[*Enter Emma, showing in Mr Pontifex*]

EMMA Mistress will be in soon, sir.

PONTIFEX Thank you, Emma. I hope you're a good girl, Emma.

EMMA I try to be, sir. [*Exit*]

PONTIFEX That's right. Let me see, what have I got down for this afternoon? The Boys' Club — O, I must not stay very long. The worst of these women is that they expect such long visits —Heigh ho! I want to do my duty and all that kind of thing — but these women — they won't leave a fellow alone — they would be making love all the day long if I let 'em. And if you give an inch they take an ell. And they are so literal. I talk about the Church in my sermons — well, one must talk about something, and I could never manage the evangelical Epistles — but they take it so seriously, they are so absurd over it! I wonder if Roman priests have the same trouble. Roman! What would poor old Dad think if he heard me talking about Roman priests. Well — well — well — we live in strange times. It seems to me that in these days we each of us live three or four separate existences. It is not that we deceive people, but each of our separate existences thinks it is the only one there is! O dear, I wish Mrs Entermore would come — I am really dreadfully hungry.

[*A ring at the bell*]

That must be the lady! Well — at any rate, I hope she'll give me some cake for tea this time.

[*Enter Emma showing in Miss Flo Donahue, most fashionably dressed*]

EMMA Mistress will be in soon, Ma'm.

FLO I beg your pardon, sir. I hope I did not interrupt.

[*She arranges her bonnet in the glass, then seats herself with a most grand air*]

PONTIFEX Not at all, Madam. Allow me to introduce myself, Madam. My name is Pontifex — Senior Curate, you know, at St Walpurga's-in-the-West.

FLO [*Aside*] This is that horrid curate, I suppose, that spoils poor Roland's life by making love to his Missus. Ugh, the black whale! 'Ee's told us all about 'im at the 'Goat and Boy'.
[*Aloud*] My name is Donahue, sir, and I have come to call upon Mrs Entermore.

PONTIFEX [*Aside*] She must be wanting a situation as Governess. How unfortunate there should be no such person as Miss Entermore. I really can't be the one to disillusion her. [*Aloud, politely*] You know this part of London?

FLO Know it, Mr Pumptext? I know every stick and stone, I know every shop and street in it. My father was a retired officer and lived in 'ammersmith, Mr Pumptext.

PONTIFEX I do not envy him, Madam. Personally I shall be glad enough to leave London. I really think I am only myself when I am among thrushes and primroses.

FLO Perhaps you hunt, Mr Pumptext?

PONTIFEX Well — no — at any rate, not now.

FLO [*Aside*] I must get in a dig at him soon — the black devil, to make love to Roland's lady!

PONTIFEX Are you, er — a — a — a Churchwoman?

FLO [*In great wrath, as though being accused of something dreadful*] No! Sir!

PONTIFEX [*Aside*] I am relieved to hear it. [*Aloud*] Isn't it a pity that you haven't got more time to think about these questions?

FLO [*Angrily*] Are you talking to me, sir? — a woman old enough to be your mother. I tell you what it is, young man — you are a spoilt boy — that's what you are — a wilful, conceited, uppish, spoilt boy. I suppose you think …

[*She looks slyly at him, sideways. Pontifex nervously edges his chair away*]

PONTIFEX [*Aside*] I knew it would come soon. I knew it would. The one thing I dread most of all — I am alone with an amorous woman.

FLO I suppose you think that I'm in love with you, like other silly people, eh?

[*Pontifex moves his chair still further off*]

All right, young man, I'm not going to hurt you. I know what you are — you're a bloomin' boy — you're nothing but a bloomin' boy. You think these ladies like Mrs Entermore take you serious, don't you? Why, they all laughs at yer, be'ind your back — they laughs at yer, Mr Pumpertext. I tell you wot it is — they mothers yer. You're a nice boy, I dessay — now I looks at you myself I sees you've a tidy bit of flesh on yer — and a smilin' come-on-aisy sort of blushin' countenance! You thinks they're a-lovin' yer an' all that, Mr Pumptext, when all the time they're motherin' yer.

[*She comes towards him as though about to kiss him, and pursues him round the chairs*]

That's wot it is — they're motherin' yer. I shouldn't mind doin' a bit of it myself.

[*The front door opens and shuts. They hear steps on the stairs and the voices of Mr and Mrs Entermore*]

Lord! 'Ere's Roland — 'ee'll never forgive me!

PONTIFEX — I think Mr Entermore will not be very pleased to see me.

FLO — What shall I do?

PONTIFEX — What shall we do?

FLO — 'Ide, yer bloomin' black beetle, 'ide!

[*She pushes Pontifex behind the curtain and draws it round them both. Enter Madeline and Roland. The curtain moves at intervals, as though Flo were embracing Pontifex and he resisting; but neither Madeline nor Roland notice it*]

ROLAND — Listen to me, Madeline. Even suppose I had flirted with a girl now and then, does that imply that I have ceased to love you? Have I not always come back to you? Come back with a sense of relief, as exchanging a transitory sensation for a permanent happiness? Believe me, my darling, these girls I have talked to — flirted with, if you like — have never really been anything to me; I have not had the remotest sentiment about them — it has been pure amusement.

MADELINE — [*With contempt*] Pure amusement!

ROLAND — But you I have always loved with my soul, with the deepest part of my being — with what is divine in me. Are you going to be jealous of a stray laugh or look or kiss even — which means nothing more than the merest transitory attraction? Come, Madeline, I will be quite honest and candid with you. All husbands, without a single exception, feel these passing desires for other women.

MADELINE Good God! What a world!

ROLAND But some of them feel so deep and so spiritual an affection for their wives that such passing emotions even when indulged, mean no more to them than bubbles upon a stream.

MADELINE [*Starting up*] Why do women submit to such a degradation?

ROLAND Partly because Society is organized to make them submit by keeping them dependent on men for their own and their children's support — and partly because of their incredible ignorance.

MADELINE You make me sick of the whole race.

ROLAND That is because you take such a material view of things. If you looked deeper you would be so gratified at having won the permanent and spiritual affection of an honourable man. You would — you would allow him these little lapses.

MADELINE Lapses!

ROLAND Look at the wives of so-called virtuous men — are they happy? I tell you there is no selfishness more repulsive than the selfishness of so-called virtuous husbands — they growl, they fume, they mutter, they sulk, they burst out and then they act the martyr — and why? Because they are repressing with a morbid violence the little venial errors that Nature indicates as wise. They are intolerable to live with — and why? Because they are always there — they never go away. I tell you, my dear Madeline, you elegant and fastidious ladies owe more than you imagine to these fringes of society. Bohemia saves Belgravia from the two most miserable of human evils.

MADELINE What evils?

ROLAND Boredom and bad temper.

MADELINE And at what a cost!

ROLAND The cost is really a mere nothing.

MADELINE How can you speak like that? You know very well that the loss of delicacy of feeling, of refinement, of sentiment, of honour, all that we have been taught to value most, must spring from associating with these base and immoral people, these designing and intriguing people.

ROLAND Who are you speaking of, Madeline?

MADELINE The women who let you — who let you — O , I can't say it!

ROLAND Who let us flirt with them, you mean — but are these women necessarily bad?

MADELINE O, I cannot bear to think of them!

ROLAND They are not so unlike yourself.

MADELINE Roland!

ROLAND They get jealous sometimes.

MADELINE They!

ROLAND And they sometimes suffer.

MADELINE Enough, Roland — you cannot expect me to believe that women such as these, blinded by every sort of depravity ...

ROLAND [*Aside*] Who is she talking about?

MADELINE ... are able to feel or to endure as much — [*Begins to cry*] — as — as — as — as I do.

ROLAND Madeline — where is Tony? He ought to be home by this time.

MADELINE O, Roland, I thought you wouldn't mind. I told Mr Pontifex he might take him to the Children's Service. It is a special service, the Children's Mass, they call it — it is a very beautiful idea. By the way, Roland, you won't mind my saying it but I'm afraid Mr Pontifex's feelings will be hurt if we don't ask him to dinner soon — I'm afraid, as it is, he thinks you dislike him.

ROLAND [*Angrily*] And haven't I cause to dislike him? You blame me for flirting with other girls — when I tell you the thing's entirely on the surface and I don't care a snap of my fingers for any of them — and all the time you're giving your soul to this priest. Yes. I say it, Madeline — your soul! O, these priests, these priests, what misery have they not caused since the foundation of the world! They do not speak of love — they do not kiss girl's lips under the mistletoe — they do not take girls to theatres or give them suppers. O, no! They only draw the very living souls out of their bodies — they only make them madly, desperately in love. They only spoil forever and ever and ever the fresh innocence of their girlish passions. O, these priests! Which do you think is most likely to interfere with the happiness of a home — a woman's surrender of her whole self — of the deepest and most sacred portion of her being — into the hands of one who is not her husband — or a man's casual flirtation with a pretty wench or two, forgotten as soon as it is indulged in, and sending him back with added tenderness to the wife from whom his deepest affections have never wavered? You are materially-minded, Madeline, else you would not hold the body of so much more importance than the soul.

MADELINE O, Roland, Roland, if you could only try to be good, too!

[*She seizes his hand*]

ROLAND [*He draws back*] I am sorry, my dear, but I cannot help associating goodness with clergymen.

MADELINE [*Rising with spirit*] And I cannot help associating evil with barmaids. I think, Roland, we won't talk any more about this now. I am going downstairs. [*As she goes*] I suppose you won't be in for dinner tonight?

ROLAND Madeline, you know I promised Florian — but perhaps — if you wish it ...

MADELINE O, no — keep your appointment. [*Exit*]

ROLAND Well! I call this too much. It's bad enough to be married at all — but to be married without any of the compensations — to be married to a — a nun! But I think I shall murder that Pontifex — I don't suppose he cares really a brass farthing about my wife —it is only his way — his innocent little way — to snatch the soul out of a woman's body and leave her husband only the skin. It is his profession, too — his celestial profession. O, he means no harm. He is doubtless a good man, a good, holy, pious man. I think I would give up the whole of this legacy to be permitted to knock his holy head off without being hung for it.

[*Exit*]

Scene 4

Mrs Entermore's Drawing Room

[*Enter Pontifex and Flo from hiding*]

FLO Well — I've heard myself called some names before,

but this beats all — a 'pure' amusement, am I? The villain, the villain —I wish I had him here. Pure amusement indeed! I'll teach him to call me 'pure'. Is 'pure' a fit title for a decent girl wot earns 'er own living. I'll 'pure' him! [*Turning in anger against Pontifex*] And as for you, you wicked man, taking advantage like that of a lady behind a curtain. I'll report you to yer superior orifices — I'll charge you — I'll call in the Court Wardens.

PONTIFEX [*Confused and agitated*] Do anything you please, my good Madam — but, for Heaven's sake, let us get out of this house before we are discovered.

FLO Well? Wot was I sayin'? Go along — I know the rules of milit-ary tackticks as well as you. D'ye think I want to stay in this bloomin' bedlam any more than you?

[*Arranges her hat once more before the glass*]

PONTIFEX [*In despair*] Hush, my dear madam. For Heaven's sake, don't make such a noise. [*Aside*] If Mrs Entermore finds me here with this woman she'll never have me in her house again; and between them they're sure to tell the Rector.

FLO What are you mee-owing about, Father Ignatius? Come on, take off your bloomin' beetle crushers and 'old 'em in your 'and. Gawd 'elp us if the front door's locked on the outside. Are we down-'earted? No!

[*Exit Flo and Pontifex*]

ACT THREE

Scene i

The home of the Entermores.

[*Mrs Entermore alone, copying church notices. The doorbell rings*]

MADELINE O, there is the bell. I am sure that Mr Pontifex will be surprised at what I have done. So many more than he expected. I have quite neglected poor, dear Roland the last few days. But I daresay he doesn't mind. [*Sighing*] He has so often left me for his friends that it is only fair I should leave him once-in-a-way.

[*Remains standing with heightened colour and flashing eyes looking fixedly at the door. Enter Pontifex*]

PONTIFEX [*Aside*] She certainly looks excited. It is extraordinary how these women fall in love with me. [*Aloud*] Ah, my dear lady! Thank you, yes, my voice has been better during the last two days. I over-strained it, I think, in the Lenten services. We poor parsons have to work when other people play. By the way, I heard rather a funny story the other day — but I won't tell it to you [*Jocularly*] till tea comes — and if I don't like your cake, you see...

MADELINE O, that reminds me: I entirely forgot how fond you are of cake. What an unfortunate thing. I don't believe there is any cake in the house. I ordered muffins.

PONTIFEX [*Jocularly*] Of course I shan't wait then. I shall go on to Mrs Heliobottom's. Muffins are dreadfully indigestible and I have to preach tonight.

MADELINE [*Holding her face with both hands, her elbows propped on the table*] You will scold me as a Priest for what I am going to say now, but I must confess to you I have forgotten what festival it is.

PONTIFEX [*Reproachfully*] Forgotten St Walpurga's! I am afraid, Missus, you haven't been reading your Church history lately.

MADELINE No, I confess it. O dear! [*She sighs deeply and sinks into profound thought*]

PONTIFEX [*In a voice partly jocose and partly sympathetic*] My dear lady! I shall have soon, as your Spiritual Director, to prescribe for you a course of the Confessional. [*Aside*] If she herself expresses a wish to build a church that will be quite a different thing of course.

[*Emma, the maid, brings tea*]

MADELINE That will do. Is there any cake in the house?

EMMA No, Miss.

MADELINE Send Dobbit out to get some.

PONTIFEX [*When the maid has gone*] That last order of yours was not on my behalf, I hope?

MADELINE [*Settling herself at the tea-table*] O, no. Three lumps, as usual? And no milk? Won't you take a muffin while they're hot?

PONTIFEX [*Eating the muffin in such a way as to make his cheeks and lips extremely greasy*] Now, let's have it, my friend: why did you sigh like that just now? Even you unaccountable dear ladies don't sigh like that for nothing.

MADELINE [*Looking away with a sort of suppressed sob*] I wish you wouldn't ask me these things in that kind of voice.

PONTIFEX [*Aside*] This is extremely embarrassing. She is evidently in love with me. I shall have to efface myself again. [*Aloud*] Well, my dear lady?

MADELINE I could not tell you except as to a priest, and it seems — it seems — rather odd, doesn't it? — over the tea-table.

PONTIFEX That is the beauty of our Church, my friend. The Romans do these things mechanically and in such an unnecessarily regal manner. We understand human nature better. We do not compel, we draw. We do not command, we attract. We do not seek, we are sought.

MADELINE The truth is, Mr Pontifex, I — I — [*Covering her face with her hands*] — O, don't look at me! I can't say it while you look at me.

PONTIFEX Calm yourself, dear — I mean, dear Mrs Entermore. I will look at that picture of 'Love and Life' over the mantelpiece.

[*He turns round*]

MADELINE What I wanted to say was — [*Getting up from her seat*] — No, I'll stand behind you and say it. O, you can see me in that glass. No, you shan't look. I'll hold your eyes. You shan't look. [*She puts her hands over his eyes. He clasps his hands tightly together*] The thing is this: I — I have found out lately that I do not love my husband as much as I used to do. And I want to ask you, is it wrong to feel this — this coldness when he makes advances to me? I have prayed about it, but it is growing worse and worse. O, sometimes when he spends whole evenings with his friends and comes home late — [*She begins to cry and bows her head*] — I am sitting up and I feel as if I almost hated him.

[*She covers her face with her hands and sits on the edge of a chair, sobbing. He rises very deliberately, arranges the plates and places his hands on her head*]

PONTIFEX Don't cry. We all have to bear these trials. Human love is a variable and uncertain thing. We cannot love when we ought to love, and we love — [*Her frame trembles with sobs*] — when we ought not to love. Divine love, on the contrary, is sure and stable. It never alters. It relieves, it fortifies, it consoles. Let us turn, my dear lady, from the tides and cross-currents of this inscrutable world and take refuge at the everlasting altars of our gracious and pitiful Mother the Church.

MADELINE I will, I will, I will. [*She falls on her knees*] O, how can I thank you enough for the help you have been to me and the divine power you have given me?

[*At this moment the bell rings. She gets rapidly to her feet. Enter Emma*]

EMMA There's a woman at the door, Madam. She's not a very respectable woman, Ma'm, asking for Master. I said he was out, and she said she might wait till he comes in. What am I to say, Ma'm?

MADELINE [*Looking appealingly at Pontifex*] Tell her it's no good — and yet — [*In a decided voice*] — no. Tell her to wait a few minutes while I think what to do.

EMMA Yes, Ma'm. [*Going*]

MADELINE And, Emma, don't let her go into any of the rooms. Give her a chair in the hall and — and — shut the kitchen door.

EMMA [*Retiring*] Yes, Ma'm.

PONTIFEX I am sorry for you, Mrs Entermore.

MADELINE [*Haughtily*] I do not need any pity. I am quite able to go my own way. I am not one of those wives who are dependent on their husbands. I have my own interests, my own friends.

PONTIFEX You certainly have one. [*Holding out his hand, which she takes and holds, while she speaks*]

MADELINE I have had enough of this sort of thing. Neglect, neglect, neglect. He tells me he goes to see his friends. How do I know where he goes? It is no use. These free-thinking and Socialistic ideas always end in this way. It is only a real, living faith, a real faith in a definite Church, that saves us from bottomless corruption. What can I do? I cannot separate myself from him for the child's sake. What can I do? [*She seizes Mr Pontifex's hand with the other as well, so that she holds him with both*] What can I do, my dear, my only earthly friend? What can I do?

PONTIFEX [*Aside*] I had made up my mind not to say a word about that new church. It was really too vulgar of old Bray to ask me. But I have found what Roland Entermore is really like. The thing becomes quite different, indeed it becomes wrong, it becomes both wrong and foolish to lose such an opportunity. [*He gently places Mrs Entermore in a chair and sits down near her. Aloud*] I realize now what you want. You want action. You want something that will occupy you and divert your mind from this distressing subject. Now, Mrs Entermore, I will speak quite plainly. I know, for you have told me yourself, that you have received lately a considerable legacy.

MADELINE What of that, Mr Pontifex?

PONTIFEX You say you want to do something for our good Mother. This is the opportunity. Mr Bray wants to build a new church in Wrench St.

[*A knock at the door*]

MADELINE Come in.

[*Enter Emma*]

EMMA The woman has gone. She said she couldn't wait any more. She left this letter for you.

MADELINE For me!

EMMA Yes, Ma'm. She wrote it in the 'all, Ma'm.

MADELINE Thank you, Emma. You can take away the tray.

[*Emma removes the tea things. Madeline holds the letter but does not open it*]

Go on. Finish what you were saying to me.

PONTIFEX I understand that this money was left to you and not your husband. [*Looks at her solemnly*] Money is a great responsibility, Mrs Entermore.

MADELINE I have half promised to let him have the larger part of it to invest in a paper he is interested in. I don't care about the paper myself, but Roland assures me that it is certain to be a great success — and, you see, I want to have something for Tony in case anything happened. [*Smiling sadly*] After all, one owes something to one's husband. He married me when I was penniless. He has supported me in luxury for seven years. I cannot very well refuse him what he asks for now.

PONTIFEX Open that letter, Mrs Entermore.

MADELINE You see, I don't know anything definitely against him, and it seems a shame, on mere suspicion...

PONTIFEX Open that letter, Mrs Entermore.

MADELINE [*Opens the letter and reads*] This is dreadful. I shan't read this.

[*She tears it across and making a gesture as though to*

throw it in the fire]

PONTIFEX May I see it?

[*Madeline looks at him with some surprise, but hands him the pieces. He puts them together and reads aloud. She listens, leaning on the back of a chair with her mouth open*]

PONTIFEX 'I hope this finds you as well as it leaves me. I make bold to tell you that my young man, Job Sw________, Sw________ ' — I can't read this — ' 'as left me to parish destitout and is living with Bess Round — bein' kep' by her, an' she's payin' 'im on Mr Roland's money. Signed, Pol Flecker. P.S. 'Ee meets 'er at the 'Goat and Boy' an' Bardolph's.'

MADELINE [*Sinking down on the sofa, hiding her face in her hands and rocking to and fro*] O, I am punished. I am punished. O, I cannot bear this. I didn't know it was as bad as this. I thought all this time he was true to me. And he is true to me! This letter must be a falsehood. O, why didn't I do what he wanted? Why didn't I let him give Tony the Bible lessons himself?

PONTIFEX [*Angrily*] I clearly see you have no longer any need for advice, Mrs Entermore. [*Looking at his watch*] It is near church time. Please excuse me if I hurry away. Good night.

MADELINE [*She takes no notice of him at all, but continues rocking herself to and fro*] O, Roland, you said you loved me. You said you loved me.

[*A ring at the bell. Enter Emma*]

I will see no-one. O, it is too late!

EMMA Mr Florian Fay.

[*Enter Florian*]

FLORIAN How do you do, Mrs Entermore. No! I won't take tea. Tea in the afternoon is most dangerous to the nerves. A drop of absinthe about four o'clock sets you up wonderfully. But really, Mrs Entermore, with your beauty and your wit you ought to be able to lead a successful revolt against tea.

MADELINE Ours is Indian, I think. I get it from the stores.

FLORIAN You ought to start a Society Against Tea. Everything nowadays is done by Societies. I sometimes think that the World itself depends upon a Society for the Propagation of Life. So that if we really could collect a sufficient number of people against it — it might be broken up.

MADELINE [*Sighing*] It would stop a great deal of misery if it were.

FLORIAN We are only miserable because we rely upon others for our happiness.

MADELINE What else is there to rely on?

FLORIAN Ourselves.

MADELINE O, that is easy to say. In real life it breaks down.

FLORIAN [*Sarcastically*] Then there is our ancient, comfortable and solidly established Church.

MADELINE [*Sighing*] I know.

FLORIAN There are her hymns.

MADELINE [*Sighing*] I know.

FLORIAN There are her psalms.

MADELINE [*Sighing*] I know.

FLORIAN There are her sacraments.

MADELINE [*Sighing*] It is true.

FLORIAN And there are priests.

MADELINE [*Looking up*] You are laughing at me, Mr Fay.

FLORIAN Not at all. I have come, on the contrary, on a mission of love.

MADELINE What do you mean?

FLORIAN A mission of love. [*Rising and bowing low*] Your husband's love, Mrs Entermore, for another woman.

MADELINE What do you mean — for another woman? Sir, this is an insult. [*Advancing towards the bell*]

FLORIAN [*Laying his hand upon her arm and speaking quickly and earnestly*] Insult or not, it is true, Mrs Entermore, but your revenge is in your own hands. Roland is anxious, or will be soon, to escape from his promise to invest money in the 'Black Pierrot'. Hitherto (I know these things, you see) you have opposed him in this. Now is your opportunity. Oppose him again. Insist, I say, insist that the money shall go where he originally proposed.

MADELINE [*Peevishly*] Sir! You don't know women. When everything else is gone, do you think we care for money?

FLORIAN Very well then. Let it go. Let him spend your money upon common women of the town. But what of your child? Will he thank you for this — this waste of what one day should be his?

MADELINE [*Wringing her hands*] O, this is too much. You all talk of money, money, money. You don't really care for my feelings at all. You don't know what it is to feel as I feel. [*Sobs*]

FLORIAN I anticipated your agitation, Madam, your justifiable agitation, and I had the forethought to bring with me — [*Produces a document from his pocket*] — a prepared paper, by signing which you invest this money of yours in the 'Black Pierrot' and make certain that your husband does not give any more away — [*He repeats this, leering at her*] — does not give any more away, at least not in such large quantities as he did last night.

MADELINE Last night?

[*She hesitates a moment and then she picks up Pol's letter*]

You are all against me and I answer you all thus —

[*She throws, into the fire, first his document, and then Pol's letter. Then she opens the door*]

Go, sir!

[*Florian exits, bowing*]

Now I await my husband.

SCENE 2

The Entermores' Drawing Room.

[*Enter Roland*]

ROLAND I cannot endure this any longer. She does nothing but pray and talk to that Pontifex. She accuses me of neglect and ill-treatment when I am only living out my life — one must live out one's life. One must be oneself. And I have done nothing to be ashamed of. I have had enough of this. What is the use of being virtuous without motive or reward? If she blames me when I do not deserve it, I swear she shall have something to blame me for. Yes, she shall, by Heaven! I'll go and see that girl of mine, that girl, Bess, this very afternoon. I will go to her lodging. I don't see why, when I am supporting her, I should only be allowed to see her in taverns and bars. I will go to her lodging.

[*Exit Roland. Enter Madeline*]

MADELINE It is a strange thing. I cannot understand it. I seem so weak and changeable. A little while ago I was complaining that I had lost my love for my husband, but now the news that he is supporting a bad woman has made me utterly miserable. The Church does not console me as it did. I feel listless even when I am listening to my friend talking about the superiority of spiritual over earthly love. I cannot tell what is the matter with me. I wish I knew exactly how far my husband goes, and whether this girl's story is true or false. I burnt the letter but I remember the address. I have almost a mind to go and see this girl myself and get the truth out of her. I can't stand this suspense, and my questions only make Roland angry and proud. Yes, I will go. Things can't be worse than they are now.

[*Exit Madeline*]

Scene 3

Rev. Bray Smith's Rectory.

[*Rev. Bray Smith and Mr Pontifex discovered talking*]

BRAY SMITH Well, my dear Pontifex, and what success in our little plan?

PONTIFEX [*Gloomily*] It is no use, Vicar. I was mistaken in Mrs Entermore. She is not so devoted to the Church as I imagined. She allows earthly passions to come between her and the Service of God.

BRAY SMITH [*Smiling*] You must turn this infatuation away from yourself and fix her mind upon other things.

PONTIFEX She has no infatuation for me.

BRAY SMITH What?

PONTIFEX I repeat it. She has no infatuation for me. No woman could endure what she has without — without losing her love for her husband. No woman except Mrs Entermore. But she has not lost it. She shows extreme jealousy.

BRAY SMITH You should have told me of all this before, Pontifex. I didn't know there were little — little episodes in this wealthy and distinguished family. It is a great pity, for they are well connected on both sides.

Scene 4

Inside Bess Round's Room.

[*A double bed. A broken washing stand*]

BESS I don't know 'ow it is, but I don't feel as though this money of Roland's 'as done me any special good. I don't go up West any more than I like, an' I 'ave my 'ot port at the pub without fear of 'avin' to go to bed on a empty stomach for neglecting business. But then, I'm no different from what I was. Respectable people look me up and down just the same in the street. And I 'ear those bloomin' shop-girls giggle wen I past 'em. An' I don't feel no different inside, 'cept as I feel down-'earted when I thinks of everything. Well, we springeth up as grass and continueth not. What must be must be and if it's to come, 'tis to come. [*She goes to the window*] O, there's Joe! And me in this mess!

[*She quickly pulls down her sleeves, ties a ribbon in her hair, slips off her skirt and puts on a bright blue one and pokes up the fire. A knock at the door. Enter Job, drunk. She goes up to kiss him. He repels her*]

JOB Wot 'ave yer got for me this evenin'? I want a couple o' quid,d'ye hear? None o' your cheek. I want a couple o' quid.

BESS O Joe, sit down, there's a good boy and let's be nice and comfortable by the fire. I've got your favourite drink ready for when the kettle boils.

[*She pulls him towards a chair by the fire. He resists, throwing her off violently*]

JOB I want that money, I tell yer. And the sooner yer let me 'ave it the better it'll be for you.

BESS But Joe, dear Joe, I've only got ten shillin's. 'Ee only gives me thirty shillin's a week and 'tis only Wednesday now and I shan't see 'im till Saturday, an' me rent's owin' out of this.

JOB O blast the rent! Let 'im pay the rent. The rent's 'is affair. You give me those two quid. Come, 'tis no use pretendin' you 'aven't got them. I know you 'ave got them. These gentlemen gives more than thirty shillin's when they're gone on a girl. I know that.

BESS But 'ee ain't gone on me. 'Ee's not like the rest of them. 'Ee's a kind of religious gent, Joe. 'Ee thinks a lot about reformin' and livin' straight and givin' up the game.

JOB [*Menacing her*] I ain't a-goin' to believe none of that.

Now then, you — divulge, young woman, or it'll be the worse for you. [*He reels about the room, searching cupboards etc*] Look here, I believe you've got that money 'idden in your bloomin' clothes. I'll 'ave it, I tell yer. I'll 'ave it if I 'ave to strip every blasted rag off your bones!

[*He advances threateningly towards her. She escapes round the table, getting frightened as he nearly catches her*]

BESS Let me alone Joe. What are you goin' to do? What are you goin' to do? I believe you want to murder me!

JOB Well, my girl, I guess it will come to something of that kind bye and bye if you don't hand over that money. Blast yer! Come 'ere! Gawd! When I do gets to yer I'll make yer pay for this.

BESS [*Throws down her purse on the table*] There's all I've got. You can see for yourself.

JOB [*Counts the contents*] Ten shillin's and ninepence. There's only ten shillin's and ninepence 'ere. You've got more money on yer than that and I'm goin' to 'ave it, yer screwy pence-pot. I'm goin' to 'ave it, by God, if I 'ave to murder yer for it. [*He purues her and gets nearer and nearer. He seizes her*] Out with that money!

BESS I 'aven't got it. O, Joe, what are you going to do with me? O, I love you Joe, it was for you.

[*Enter Pol*]

POL Give it 'er Jobie. That's right! 'It 'er 'ard, Jobie!

[*Job drops Bess and they both turn towards Pol*]

JOB Wot do you want 'ere?

BESS Clear out of this. We don't want none of your 'elp. We

can settle our own affairs, Jobie and I. Can't we, Jobie?

JOB [*To Bess*] You 'old yer tongue, can't yer.

POL [*To Bess*] O 'ee's been birchin' yer, as 'ee, 'cos you don't give 'im enuff of yer bloomin' chink. Little good you've got by takin' away my boy from 'is rightful gal. 'Ee don't care nothin' for nothin' but yer chink. Don't yer make no bloomin' doubt about that. 'Ee was always sweet on me — an' 'ee's sweet on me still, 'ee is. Yes, pale face, yer can make faces and cuss as much as yer like, but 'ee's sweet on me still. D'ee 'ear that? 'Ee's sweet on me still. [*She comes towards Bess and shouts these words tauntingly, and then puts her arm round Job*] Ain't yer, old boy?

BESS [*Standing erect, her eyes flashing fire*] 'Ow dare you come here like that? 'Ow dare you come between me and my bloke? 'Ow dare you touch 'im? [*Clasps his free hand in hers*] O, Joe, Joe, put 'er out. Joe, say yer don't want 'er, Joe, and yer can go on beatin' me like a dog, Joe, only, put her out. O, I loves yer Joe. I loves yer. [*She sobs on her hand*]

POL Don't yer notice, Jobie. She's a ruddy cryin' soft, she is. Yer come 'ome with me, Jobie. Look 'at 'er. She's no better than a silly. She's a thing.

BESS [*Looking up through her tears*] I ain't a thing! [*Sobs*] I don't 'ave to —'ave to earn my livin' on the streets as some do. I won't be called a thing by anyone livin'.

JOB 'Old yer bloomin' tongues, both of yer. I think yer both bloomin' drunk.

BESS O, Joe, dear Joe, send 'er away, send 'er away and I'll let you beat me as 'ard as you like, and I won't scream out an' I won't run away s'elp me Jesus, I won't.

POL [*Putting her arms round Job and drawing him towards her and kissing him*] Come on, Jobie. Leave that silly, pesterin' mad girl there an' come 'ome with me again. I've got a nice little fire in my grate and I've got — Jobie — I — I've got ... [*She looks extremely cunning and whispers in his ear*]

BESS Don't listen to her. If you go I shall kill myself. She can't love yer as much as I do. O, Jobie, I love yer. I can't live without yer.

JOB [*Shaking them both away*] Hold yer tongues, both of you. This is a nice scene for a man to put up with. Good Lord! Yer lead a fellow a dog's life, you two gals with yer catterwauling and your messin' around. Look 'ere. Can't yer live, both of yer, in this 'stablishment? Between yer, God slop me, yer ought to make a tidy sum.

[*Bess remains on the floor and then gets slowly up and walks to the window*]

POL Don't talk nonsense, Jobie, but come back with me. I've got ... [*She whispers*]

JOB Well, I don't know but wot I won't give yer another trial, Pol. Yer can sing a fellow to sleep and talk lively, while with 'er 'tis nothin' but a lot of lovin'.

[*He advances to the door with Pol*]

BESS Jobie! [*She speaks in a strange voice. They both turn and look at her a little startled*] Jobie, the moment yer foot is over that doorstep I'll throw myself out this winder!

POL Come on, Jobie. Never mind 'er. She won't throw 'erself out of no window. Don't you think it.

JOB [*He hesitates*] It's 'er own bloomin' fault if she does.

[*They go. Bess waits till she sees them some way down the street*]

BESS O, I love 'im. I love 'im. O, my 'eart is broke. I can't live like this. [*She starts wildly*] I thought I 'eard my old mudder callin' me. Mudder! [*She throws herself out of the window*]

Scene 5

Bess Round's room.

[*A corpse lying on the bed, with a shawl over the face. Enter Florian and Theophilus*]

THEOPHILUS This is the room. I have been here several times.

FLORIAN Well, it isn't exactly the place an artist would select for his amours, but you philosophers have curious tastes.

THEOPHILUS [*Surlily*] Don't try and be funny, Florian.

FLORIAN I hope the girl won't be long. What are we to say to her? Do you think anything we can say will persuade her to help us to secure Roland's money?

THEOPHILUS [*Sulkily*] Fool! Don't you see? If she was to threaten Mrs Entermore to swear in a court of law that the first little street brat she could lay her hands on was her's and Roland's, out of fear of a scandal Mrs Entermore would let us have the money.

FLORIAN So we are to appear in our true colours, Theo, at last.

THEOPHILUS As you please.

FLORIAN And yet it goes against the grain with me to play our friend such a scurvy trick. If it wasn't for the 'Black Pierrot', a paper likely to produce such remarkable results, and to have such an influence, I — I really don't know that I wouldn't give your pretty scheme to the devil.

THEOPHILUS You are a hypocritical fool!

FLORIAN And haven't you any compunction in persuading this girl to perjure herself on our behalf.

THEOPHILUS Compunction! Why, these girls are made of lies. They breathe lies, they drink lies, lies are their true element. Don't you waste any of your fine sentiment, my friend, on these girls. They have no affections, they have no aspirations; they are simply automata.

FLORIAN They are certainly the basis of our civilisation.

THEOPHILUS I tell you, they are lower than animals. They are utterly outside consideration. They are only useful as playthings.

FLORIAN Poor playthings!

[*Enter Mr Pontifex, who has never seen either of them before*]

PONTIFEX [*Opening the door*] Excuse me. Does Miss Bess Round live here?

FLORIAN We are — are expecting her any moment. Is this — er — an appointment, sir?

PONTIFEX [*Angrily*] What do you mean?

FLORIAN Well, naturally, considering the avocation of the lady whose lodging you have invaded, anyone might think ...

THEOPHILUS And will think, no doubt.

PONTIFEX I am an unworthy member of our Good Mother the Church. The truth is, gentlemen, that if I have any more insults from you, I'll knock you both into a cocked hat.

FLORIAN You have really a most charming colour when you get excited, sir.

THEOPHILUS You look like the original Fighting Parson.

PONTIFEX Enough! No more of this nonsense. I know the sort of people you are. Shabby-genteel people, demi-semi-mondain people.

FLORIAN What do you call us?

PONTIFEX I call you and your friend, sir, paid bullies of a woman of the very lowest class, a wretched woman, a woman who lives in the most infamous manner, a woman abandoned to drink, and, moreover, a woman who by her unscrupulous intrigues is even now drawing large sums of money from a misled and misguided gentleman. You, sir, may have, for all I know, your own share in this infamous transaction. If so, I will...

[*Enter Flo Donahue*]

FLO Well, and 'ows my little Bessie? Lord! You is entertainin' visitors, Bessie, and none of 'em strangers to me either. 'Ow do ye do, Mr Fay. Good evening, Mr Groteus. Why, bless my wig, if this ain't my own blackcoat pal, Pumptext, turned up again! You needn't be too proud to shake hands, Mr Pumptext. O, don't be distress't at my findin' you 'ere visitin' our little friend, Bessie. Young men will be young men, Mr Pumptext. I forgive them. I knows they can't 'elp it. I knows 'ow difficult they find it to resist, Mr Pumptext. But, oh, you naughty, naughty boy! [*She leers and pokes him*]

[*The voice of Roland is heard outside talking to Sue*]

ROLAND Dead! Do you say 'dead'? But why did you let these

people in?

SUE [*Sadly*] I couldn't help it, Sir.

[*Enter Roland. Sue follows him in*]

ROLAND I cannot understand why you have all come here to make your vulgar jokes over a poor dead girl who in life none of you treated with even the kindness you would use towards animals. Except you, Flo; you were kind to her.

FLORIAN Dead!

PONTIFEX I hope you realize, Mr Entermore, that I had not the slightest idea ...

[*Sue goes up to the bed and uncovers the face of the dead girl. Roland goes to the bed and kisses the girl's forehead, then he kneels down and bursts into tears*]

THEOPHILUS [*Sneering*] This is quite a dramatic scene.

FLORIAN Hush, Theo! Poor girl. Well, I have never done her any harm. Poor girl. [*Aside*] And if she had lived she would have saved the 'Black Pierrot'!

PONTIFEX I am sorry I said what I did of this poor girl. After all, she's dead now and she was a woman.

[*Goes up to the bed and raises his hand*]

Requiem ei dona eternam
perpetuum luceat et ...

FLO O dear, I shall have hysterics soon. I shall fall! Catch me!

[*Pontifex catches her. Enter Madeline*]

FLORIAN Good heavens, Mrs Entermore!

THEOPHILUS Our cue's villainous melancholy and a sigh like Tom o'Bedlam.

FLO — 'old me, Mr Pumptext.

MADELINE — [*Looking round and seeing Roland and the dead body*] Roland, Roland, what is this?

ROLAND — [*Rises and goes to her*] That is the poor girl I have been helping. She is beyond anyone's help now.

MADELINE — O, Roland, how dreadful. How did she die?

SUE — Doctor sez she must 'ave fallen out of window, Ma'm, or 'ave received a severe blow.

MADELINE — Roland, I ask you for the sake of my peace of mind, there was nothing between you and that girl that you need have been ashamed of?

FLORIAN — [*Aside to Theophilus*] O, the woman, the woman, moralistic even in the presence of death!

THEOPHILUS — [*Aside*] She is not moral, she is jealous.

FLORIAN — [*Aside*] Jealous of the dead?

THEOPHILUS — [*Aside*] Most of all, the dead.

ROLAND — I give you my word of honour that nothing ever passed between us that I am ashamed of now.

MADELINE — [As *Mr Pontifex guides Flo to a chair*] What are Mr Pontifex and that person doing? Is anything the matter with her?

FLO — O, I shall fall! I shall fall! 'old me, my darling Mr Pumptext.

ROLAND — Never mind them. [*He leads her to the bed and holds her hand*] Let us now, in the presence of this poor dead child, make up our minds to live no more, as we have done, separated, isolated lives, but to join together in doing what we can to make the fate of the unhappy and the unfortunate lighter.

FLORIAN There goes the last chance of the 'Black Pierrot'.

THEOPHILUS Don't be too cast down, my friend, he will have changed his mind tomorrow.

PONTIFEX There goes the last chance of the church in Wrench St.

FLO Good resolutions is as good resolutions does, ain't they, Percy?

MADELINE Yes, Roland, we will do as you say. I have been to blame as well as you. I now see, when brought face to face with death, the unimportance of the things I was beginning to hold dearer than your love. God speaks to us both from the life of this poor girl. Henceforth we must devote our lives to one another and our money to the cause of the poor. I have treated you unsympathetically, Roland. I have been led astray as to the real value of your love. All that is changed now entirely. Henceforth I give myself up to you. I thought I was strong. I find I am as weak as the rest.

PONTIFEX Stop and think, Madeline Entermore, before you commit yourself finally to such a scheme. Is the necessity of our Mother the Church nothing to you any more?

FLORIAN Stop and think, Roland Entermore, before you waste your time upon such a hopeless task. Is the future of the 'Black Pierrot' nothing to you any more?

FLO Don't be a blasted couple of fools, you two. You look arter yourselfs and cuddle that little boy o' yers and enjoy yourselves and leave God Almighty alone to look after the starvin' ideots wot is the work of 'is bloomin' 'ands.

THEOPHILUS Leave them alone. The best place in the world to make resolutions that are to last forever is over the body of the dead.

MADELINE [*Warning them off*] Back, all of you! Henceforth, my husband and I choose our own path for ourselves. Henceforth, his path shall be mine.

ROLAND I am afraid, Florian, the 'Black Pierrot' must get on without help from me.

MADELINE I am afraid, Mr Pontifex, you must find another patron for your church, another pupil for yourself.

ROLAND Come then, my darling, let us go. Farewell, Bessie, you have saved two souls, at any rate.

MADELINE [*Stooping down and kissing her forehead*] And they will save more!

PONTIFEX What a saint lost to the Church!

FLORIAN What a poet lost to the Muses!

THEOPHILUS What actors lost to the stage!

FLO Well, at any rate, I've 'ad enuff of this an' I shouldn't be surprised if some other ladies and gentlemen in the 'ouse 'ave 'ad enuff thinkin', too, only they don't like to show it. Come on, Percy! [*Seizes Mr Pontifex*] Who's going to come and give me a drink?

THE END

A NOTE ON THE TEXT

There appears to be no final, fair copy of the text of 'The Entermores' and the manuscript, which is untitled, is contained, in rather jumbled form, within five notebooks in the Powys collection of Syracuse University. An additional, newly discovered scene (Act Three, Scene Five) is to be found in Powys's *Cambridge and Southwick Journals* of 1890–96, but, on the basis of internal evidence, cannot be contemporary with the other material contained in these journals. For reasons which I have elaborated in my essay *John Cowper Powys, Margaret and Lily: The Evidence of the Syracuse Manuscripts* (London: Cecil Woolf, The Powys Heritage Series, Number 1, 1998) this highly autobiographical play was probably written in 1905.

Powys refers to the socialist weekly magazine *The Clarion*, which was edited by Robert Blatchford and ran from 1891 to 1932. One of the founding editors of *The Clarion* was E. F. Fay, but it seems extremely unlikely that he was a model for Florian Fay, whose magazine 'The Black Pierrot' seems more like *The Yellow Book*.

John Cowper Powys had hoped, it seems, that his play would be performed in 1905. There is no evidence that this amateur production ever took place. There was, however, a dramatised reading of the play at the Powys Society Conference in 1994, which was directed by Christopher Wilkinson and led by John Cowper's godson, the late Oliver Wilkinson, in whose memory the play has now been published.

P.R.

COMMENTARY

Reading 'The Entermores' and re-reading Paul Roberts's study, *John Cowper Powys, Margaret and Lily*, makes me feel a little sheepish. How easy it is to write critical books and articles based on material that is already published, and to confine one's commentary to work that has received its share of critical attention from other people. But any deep understanding of an author's roots and creative development must derive from what he or she has discarded, experimented with, or aborted; and material of that kind is only made available to us by the labours of genuine scholars, those who travel to view dispersed collections in distant libraries, who decipher manuscripts and re-assemble what has been set down on scraps of paper, the backs of letters or even, in some rare cases, paper bags. It depends on transcribers, cataloguers and curators. It is a dedicated person who undertakes such tasks, and it is on their work that any enlightened assessment of an author's achievement is based.

In the instance of John Cowper Powys, as Roberts has recorded, there is an enormous amount of early written work which never saw the light. That his two books of early poems did so was due to his father's financial help; nor is it really surprising, that even publishers in the Edwardian period were reluctant to print stories such as the gruesome 'Romer Mowl' and the other tales collected by Dr Bernard Jones in 1974. John Cowper was too soaked in literature for his own good, and struck attitudes long after they had ceased to be fashionable: even his first two published novels have not shaken off the influence of the 'nineties. By the time he wrote *Wolf Solent*, however, instead of being dogged by his literary influences he had learned how to wrestle with them and exploit them; his work thereafter resembles a giant (a sceptically self-denigrating giant) arising out of a heap of discarded chains. And yet much that is most disturbing in his accounts of human psychology has its origin in those derivative early writings — writings such as this play 'The Entermores'.

John Cowper is so immediately identified with lengthy novels and prolix lecture-room prose that his association with the theatre and desire to succeed in it comes as a surprise — and a surprise not merely that he should write plays at all but at his ability to compress his style sufficiently to meet the requirements of the stage. Both 'The Idiot' and *Paddock Calls* belong to the period of his early novels and are most fruitfully read in conjunction with them; 'The Entermores', however, belongs to the largely unchronicled years of his early married life. Those years are graphically portrayed in *Autobiography*; but 'portrayed' is not the same thing as 'chronicled', and it is therefore in a biographical context that one can most usefully approach this play.

The personal references are almost painfully obvious: the very opening exchange between Madeline and Roland Entermore would seem to reflect the marital tensions one deduces from John Cowper's and Margaret Powys's very different standards and preoccupations — more so, I would think, than does the posthumously published novel, *After My Fashion*. Or is the character of Nelly Moreton an act of reparation on John Cowper's part for the portrait of Madeline Entermore? The latter certainly belongs to the number of outraged avenging mother-goddess figures who haunt the contemporary pages of E. M. Forster and, more humorously presented, Oscar Wilde — purveyors of lofty religious sentiment combined with a reproachful emotionalism which invariably wrong-foots the eternal schoolboy in the male. Powys is in fact remarkably generous to Madeline in this play, and the final scene (which contrives to echo both Hardy's novel *A Pair of Blue Eyes* and Ibsen's tragic drama *Little Eyolf*) leaves her in a stronger position than before. One can understand from 'The Entermores' a little more about John Cowper's readiness to become the financial provider for women who had — or who made — claims upon him. They were magnates who had to be propitiated.

The play also reflects a side of his life which is more evasively described in *Autobiography* — his relations with the prostitute Lily. Women of easy virtue (to use that alluring contemporary designation) made a natural appeal to the guilt-ridden and inhibited sons of late Victorian sexual strictness. Powys gives a delightful account of Lily, who so improbably but indisputably accompanied him to his brother Bertie's wedding (I would love to have witnessed the purchase of that hat); one hopes — indeed assumes — that she was a more presentable and agreeable companion than are the assortment of drabs (the out-dated term comes unavoidably to mind) presented in 'The Entermores'. As to Roland's reformist ideals, they echo those of William Ewart Gladstone — not to mention the Rector of Stiffkey, that unhappy Norfolk clergyman so very different from the respectable Donnes and Johnsons of the Powys ancestry. But Roland's ideals also objectify a tension in John Cowper himself.

The prostitute was a figure who, in Victorian literature, acted almost as a sin-bearer, laden with the complex burdens of sexual, social and economic guilt — witness Dickens's wellnigh hysterical account of Martha in *David Copperfield* or Mrs Gaskell's more intelligent but still emotional portrayal of Esther in *Mary Barton*. As to Rossetti's 'Lazy laughing languid Jenny / Fond of a kiss and fond of a guinea', she is located among the sexual fantasies of the club-man's ambience, that fictitious underworld of forbidden fruits, unspeakable vices and all the stock in trade of the sweets of sin, which provided such nervous undercurrents in Powys's early writings until they are triumphantly exposed and debunked in the portraits of Urquhart and Tilly-Valley in *Wolf Solent*. In 'The Entermores' one sees an early instance of such a corrective view: Flo and Poll and Bess Round (whose name is to be used again in *Wolf Solent*) are vigorous earthy women who have none of the deadly sweet eroticism of Powys's sylph-like temptresses, which no doubt was to be purveyed in the pages of 'The Black Pierrot'. Their language constantly subverts the high-falutin' exchanges between the principal characters, and Flo, by rounding off this play with her 'Who's going to come and give me a drink?' anticipates the saving cup of tea which brings that novel to its sober and sobering conclusion. 'The Entermores', with its defiant anti-clericalism and down-to-earth treatment of its 'fallen women' shows that Powys was never entirely at the mercy of the morbid literary imaginings that afflicted him.

It is in this connection that 'The Entermores' throws such valuable light on the question of what kind of an author John Cowper Powys at this time wished to be. In such a play as this he hoped to attract a degree of popular attention, just as stories like 'Romer Mowl' were aiming to do. But this kind of material seems designed more to arouse and frighten himself than the intellectual reading public his ambitions hoped to reach. 'The Black Pierrot', with its echoes of *The Yellow Book*, represented in fact everything that Powys in his maturity was to reject. And it is not the least significant thing about 'The Entermores' that it contains not a trace of that response to natural forces and to landscape which were to provide the mature artist both with a theme and a vehicle for self-liberation. The distance between this play and a romance like *Porius* seems to be as great as those between the various planets of his final fictions.

Glen Cavaliero

JOHN COWPER POWYS

The New Paganism
An Ethical Essay

It must be admitted that man has developed during the last two thousand years. He is still a rapacious, malicious and envious animal, but he is not quite what he was. Christianity and the new science and democracy which have sprung up under the shadow of Christianity have made some changes. It is perhaps in the moral world that the change has been most prolific in happy results.

Most potent of all the passions, most necessary of all the emotions that affect our lives, the sexual instinct has undergone a complete transformation. Before the Classic world was destroyed this instinct was permitted to advance unimpeded to its furthest limit. Associated, as it must ever be, with the inexplicable allurements of beauty, consecrated so in an art that gave permanence to all transitory and exquisite things, this phallic cult, by the audacity of its own excess and daring, fell upon weariness, ennui and disillusion. Desire, permitted its full riot, proved the worst enemy of the very ecstasy it sought, and in the rapid creation of ever-new objects of pursuit exhausted the very well-spring from which it drew its charm and its attraction. The sublime asceticism associated with the personality of Jesus found itself at once in harmony with an inevitable reaction of Nature herself against this deplorable waste of the waters of life. And though in Jesus this reaction took a peculiar form — the only form, perhaps, through which it could affect mankind at large — yet in the finer spirits of the old regime changes had begun and some have wondered whether, if it had been brought about without the triumph of the Barbarians and the shaking, if not the overthrow, of the ancient order, it would not have been better and happier for the world. But such speculations have little value. In the history of humanity we have not to consider the Possible or the Advisable or the Ideal, but simply what happened. This is our one criterion for the present, our one witness for the future. The fact remains that Jesus possessed himself of the Pantheon; that the Roman system was taken over by the new spirit and entirely transformed, that the gods became saints, the temples churches and an unearthly Pharos of spiritual glory fixed its lamp against the raging waters of natural lust.

More and more have those waters been curbed and chastened under the protection of this benignant light fed with sacred oil. A great promontory has been raised up against the outer deep, and there our ships have ridden long in calm and safety.

But the miraculous insight of Jesus has been shown in nothing so much as in his perception of the essential unity of body and soul. In the earlier and in the later world there have been fierce reactions against the natural animalism of man. Such reactions, dividing into hard dualism things which are of one origin, seeking to separate the sap from the branch and the bark from the wood, have proved ever ineffectual and unhappy. The Christian consecration of the body by its audacious doctrine of the resurrection and by the sacramental principle has been, in reality, the main secret of its success. Here it has shown itself wiser than the Idealists and wiser than the Bacchanalia against which the Idealists protested. The passions and desires of the flesh are only to be held as evil when not caught up and inspired by the higher emotions. It is no longer a matter of war between body and soul — body has become spiritualized and spirit has become incarnate. And in this fortunate appeal to the unity of all things, in this happy insistence upon the inherent wickedness of extremes, Christianity has found a path upon which it may go far without exhausting its power.

The sexual instinct is not to be held as simply evil — it is to be taken up and reaffirmed by the very passion that itself has given birth to it. Love is to be at once a new sanction and a new restraint — *Ama et fac quod vis*. But whilst this is so it must not be forgotten that in its impassioned reaction against the old excesses (that produced the old ennui) Christianity is not always true to its wiser self.

Rome has always had a tendency to crush life into inflexible grooves. Protestantism, the most pernicious of heresies, has always trampled on the subtle compromises that Nature delights in taking such trouble to evolve, and it is partly because of the recent tendency of Christianity to divide itself into rigid Authority on the one hand and loose and vulgar Independence on the other that humanity has become more and more convinced that if it is to give its name to the new development of the human spirit, it must reorganize itself very rapidly.

What Catholicism has done cannot be undone, any more than what the Classic world did, but no-one must dogmatically assert that because so special a good luck helped it to hit upon its name that therefore it will be permitted to enclose the universe. No doubt, as recent apologists assert, the faith does not necessarily fall because history disproves its miracles and science antiquates its theology, but unless the faith shows that it can develop internally and in essence to answer the ever-new demands of life, it must hand over its rich deposit of accumulated spiritual spoils to some other system and some other form.

And it is in regard to sexual freedom that this new demand of life is now primarily coming to be made.

The old paganism vanished because in its lust it destroyed pleasure, but may not a new paganism arise — nay! be already risen — which, while recognizing what Christianity has done by its apotheosis of love and its rejection of the other, recognize also that there was something of freedom, of variety, of demonic mystery and primitive earth-wisdom about the old cults that has been lost and forgotten in the change. Science and metaphysics — nay, religion itself! — compel us to regard the flesh as being as mysterious and wonderful as the spirit: as being, in fact, but another mode of the same elementary force. Is it not then likely that the cult that has for its aim so passionate and abandoned a service of beauty, may offer to its diligent votaries ecstasies and ardours which are not only concealed from, but totally misunderstood by, the profane? Christianity, when it first appeared, was regarded in the ancient world as scandalous and immoral. All new sensations of a rare and exquisite character are irritating to the conventional world in which they arise and to the external routines to which they are so profoundly opposed. Whatever Christianity may essentially be, the conventional creed always utters its absurd condemnations in the language of the established creed: the spirit of the creed itself may be much more in harmony with the revolution than the routine, but it is through oracular lips that officialdom delights to curse.

And what are the practical directions in which what we have modestly called the New Paganism may be expected, or rather (for these things are matters of experiment not of theory) has already begun to advance? In the first place, in the direction of freer intercourse between the sexes. Whatever asceticism has done, the Christian Ideal of the Holy Family must be admitted to have failed. In Protestant countries this Ideal has been degraded into a gross and unlovely domesticity — in Catholic countries it has existed side by side with a childish and superstitious sensuality. Compared with the attitude of the medieval or modern world towards sexual relations, how fresh, how natural seems to us what we can gather of the attitude of the Greeks. Put a naked goddess of Praxiteles side by side with a draped female of Botticelli or Burne-Jones and who does not feel that, whatever the intellectual or moral advantage may be, the bodies of the latter are essentially morbid and impure?

Nor need even those who find in the barriers and restraints introduced by Christianity an incentive rather than an obstacle to the play and colour of passion be alarmed at the change which is occurring. A thousand causes make impossible any real return to the pure simplicity of the Greeks or to the corrupt ingenuity of the Romans. Those who insist that upon the Law of Contrast depends the whole pleasure of life and who draw the conclusion that the preservation of conventional morality and middle-class obtuseness is necessary to give edge to the individual's aberrations from both, may remain quite assured. The thing which is the foil to our finer pleasure need not exist in overpowering disproportion: and even though, which is nearly inconceivable, a freer and more subtle mode of life became universal, we shall be quite safe in assuming that other modes, compared with which even that which we shall the have attained will look narrow and rigid, must appear upon the horizon's edge.

And, after all, it is more than probable that the naïve sensuousness which, partly by reason of the inevitable nature of the fragments of their art which we possess, out of which time has extinguished all traces of colour, we attribute to them is by no means the whole of Greek life. It has been suggested that if all were known, a much nearer and more intimate connection than we have any idea of would display itself between what is now called Decadence and the life of the ancient Greeks. Even though the grossness and brutality of the Roman Empire was the outcome of the laudable Greek worship of the body, and even though Christianity in suppressing the old paganism has suppressed much that is valuable with it, we need not fear that the attempt to pick up the threads that have been dropt will in any sense be a precise return to the past — you cannot annul the influence of nineteen hundred years.

What we have now to deal with is not contrary and conflicting Utopias or theories as to what man ought to be, but simply the right interpretation of what man is. Surveying in this mood the present tendencies of society in Europe and America no one can deny that the breaking up of the old supernatural faith has been followed by greater sexual laxity. The moralist's catchword just now is to blame this laxity chiefly in regard to its effect on the increasing population. But it may reasonably be questioned whether, when once the empty spaces of the world have been occupied, there remains any particular advantage in increasing the population at the old rate. The struggle for existence from which progress proceeds may conceivably, as the social machine becomes better organized and science makes the attainment of the necessities of life easier, be thrown upon a higher plain. The keeping up of the struggle by the mere brute weight of numbers seems at once a foolish waste of energy and an unnecessary cause of suffering. This likeliest reason for the Puritanism of progressive races being put aside, it remains to be seen what other effects are likely to ensue from the freer intercourse between the sexes which we see around us.

Conventional opinion, depending on the complacent and comfortable conditions of middle-class existence, speaks with bated breath of the vice which it observes in the life of the lower and upper classes. From the point of view of saints and philosophers, of St. Francis and

Goethe, the conditions represented by this vice are infinitely more amenable to the higher emotions of the soul than those which surround the existence of the prosperous tradesman. It was not for nothing that Jesus made his appeal to the harlots when the middle-class world of his day neglected him. After all, life cannot be measured by mere continuance of health or well-being. The prostitute may die miserably at thirty and the draper's wife live comfortably till a hundred, but in a day the former (Poll Tosspot) has experienced more emotion, known more of the primal creative ecstasy that builds the world than the latter (Mrs Toad-in-a-hole) has spread over thirty years.

That a life so near to the permanent substratum of our being, a life so spontaneous, so profoundly free at once from monotony and affectation should be better than the one which we know too well hardly needs to be proved. It is well known that the only women that poets and artists feel really at home with — to say nothing of saints — are the women of the street. And this is not only because the others are so cold and so formal but because they have got so disassociated from reality, they have got by reason of their contemptible virtue so artificial, that it is rapidly becoming impossible to have anything to do with them. The middle-class 'lady' with her dissenting Ministers or Anglican Clergymen — her intolerable servants and more intolerable children — God! We turn from her with a sense of indescribable relief to Skipping Jenny or the Countess of Lesbos. The sort of artificiality which 'respectable' women display is of much grosser character and much more injurious than the airy nothings of Society. Society people candidly hunt night and day for pleasure — some of them find it and some of them miss it. They live the life of butterflies, but at least they live. Whitechapel 'Arriet candidly works all day that she may have pleasure in the evening. She lives a life of squalid drudgery varied with Bacchanalian debauch, but she lives. O droll and absurd race of respectable mortals, when will ye cease to draw your blighting curtain of colourless mediocrity round the grey and tragic nakedness of man?

But the real limitation of the point of view of conventional morality is that it substitutes a provincial for a universal interpretation of life. Individualists like Byron or Rousseau or Nietzsche may be condemned from the point of view of a universal criticism, but they cannot be condemned from the point of view of a provincial criticism. The assertion of the individual's pride and pleasure as the ultimate authority may be limited when regarded from the standpoint of the totality of things, but regarded from the standpoint of middle-class convention it appears profoundly and inherently wise.

Universal criticism cannot escape from the necessity of considering the established moral valuations of the past and the conventional moral valuations of the future; it cannot escape the necessity of eternally modifying what the present offers in relation to these.

Morality cannot even be called absolute in regard to the individual and relative in regard to the race, for all the very modifications which change its nature for the race must primarily be the work of individuals. No advantage is gained by the doctrine that things or feelings or actions are good and evil in themselves. What is happening is the gradual substitution for morality of casuistry or expediency. But will this be strong enough to restrain the brutal and the ignorant? Will this be efficacious to defend the weak? We answer this by asking, has the old morality protected the weak? Is it not true, on the contrary, that as the world becomes less 'moral' in the supernatural sense, it becomes more 'human' in the natural sense? As far as the brutal and the cruel are concerned it is not to morality, but to the law that we must look. For even remembering the necessity of all things and the essential irresponsibility of the worst criminal, it is by an equal necessity that Society protects itself. Well! Let Society protect itself — let the law be as rigid as it will. There is always the margin, the borderland, in man's life where he is under the delusion that his actions are free and where his actions one way or the other cannot be reached by the law. This is the field from which the old morality seems likely to be about to disappear.

The human race, this experiment of an experiment, is through the lives of its children experimenting every hour. Morality is but a name for a hasty synthesis of modes of conduct which experience has hit upon and, as experience changes, this hasty synthesis must change with it.

It is impossible that so dominating an idea as that of personal immortality or personal existence after death should have failed to modify in multiform ways man's view of the purpose of his life. When this idea ceases to operate, and it appears as though both metaphysics and science have pronounced its doom, it is unbelievable but that what is called morality should profoundly change.

If the pleasures of the man are still to be subjected to the pleasures of the spirit it must be on the ground not of the permanence of the one compared to the transitoriness of the other (for the individual, both are alike transient), but on the more exquisite pleasure-giving capacity of the latter here and now. Shall we get rid of the old theological tyranny only to fall under a tyranny worse than the former?

When Matthew Arnold calls upon us to give up a Personal God and bow down before a Stream of Tendency which makes for righteousness, when Mr John Morley, after telling us to resign ourselves to the last appalling stroke of annihilation, warns us that the Moral Code is more inflexible than the Christian Code — when George Eliot, having got rid of Immortality and Divinity calls upon us to abase ourselves before the eternal conception of Duty, we may well look back with longing to that creed in which the new liberty of the children of God has taken the place of the old law and in which if all things are not expedient, all things are lawful!

Nothing indeed shows more clearly the amazing insight of Jesus (Him we may still call 'Our Lord') than the intuitive refusal of the human mind having once realized His principle of *Ama et fac quod vis* to return to the empty husks of Duty and Morality. Agnostic moralists speak of the importance of subordinating the individual to the race — of the duty we are under of sacrificing our individual pleasures to the permanent happiness of the race! What is this phantom, this idol, this monster we are to offer ourselves up as sacrifices to? According to the Hegelian catchword, which is responsible for half the mistake, the human race is spoken of as an organism. Now if, by a very loose metaphor, a race can be regarded as an organism at all it is an organism that only thinks and feels and enjoys in the individual members that compose it — and why, we ask, are the individual members now alive less important than the individual members which will be alive in three hundred years?

When these people talk of the Great Organism of the Human Race they try and deceive the minds of the simple by a phrase. There is no such thing as an Over-Soul or Divine Idea which links together Past and Future in itself by thinking, feeling and being.

When we use such expressions we are using figurative — I will not say poetic — language and it is to figments of this kind that we are to sacrifice ourselves? What is the value of the Eternal Idea of the Solidarity of the Human Race compared with the red blood in one child's lips?

All these high-sounding notions are but pale shadowy attendants upon the Real. Those who enunciate these do not really believe in them — and no-one acts differently because of them. There is more truth in one superstition sprung naturally from the soil than in all these ghosts. Catholicism, with its images, its saints, its indulgences, understands humanity much better.

There is only one thing in the world that is really valuable, only one thing that completely explains itself and justifies itself by existence alone. From theories about life we must ever turn to Life itself.

All speculative thought is of the nature of negation. The normal man loves and suffers and enjoys and the normal man is right. Right, profoundly right, is the instinct that compels the normal man, the average sensual man, to refuse to sacrifice a single moment of real pleasure for the exigencies of the Race.

Nature may well groan with indignation if, after evolving with infinite trouble so exquisite a happiness-giving instrument as the human frame — after surrounding it with a thousand subtle associations and recondite charms — she sees each generation of living men and women put laboriously aside the enjoyment of so immense a gift in order that an Ideal, a monster without teeth, may chew eternally ideal husks that have no existence.

But fortunately Nature is too strong and while life lasts men eat and drink and love, knowing in their hearts, whatever the moralists say, that tomorrow they will die. Again, how hollow — how cruel — is the pressure of the vast weight of suffering that the world groans under to take away even the smallest of compensatory joys? Wise was he — that pitiful and most subtle of humanists, who exclaimed when the dead men lectured him (moralists have ever the skeleton grin) with their odious truisms that as they are now, so he must shortly be. 'Not so shortly, friends, as you suppose. Meanwhile, I am alive — I move about!'

The old religions had a truer view of the value of life. God to them was a concrete fact, not a Stream of Tendency. Who but the ever-living one, the God of Israel, gave an actual and real enlargement of the sense of existence?

Quia non infernus confitebitur tibi, neque mors laudabit te, non expectabunt qui descendunt in lacum, veritatem tuam.

The Idealists, or those who would reduce to a shadow what is real and establish as real what is a shadow, appeal to tradition for their support. Have we not also a tradition? Side by side through the ages run the two interpretations, the two visions — and if Idealism has its history, Realism has its history too. What we seek is the reconciliation, the unity that must include these opposites. And we find it in the movement and play of the soul when some concrete object instinct with implicit beauty arrests and absorbs the senses. What the mystics in all ages have sought — the hedonists in all ages have sought likewise — the desire of the mind is for life; life alone — not spirit or body — satisfies this impassioned thirst.

The mistake that moralists make is to substitute the means for the end. Morality is only a prudence, an economy by which the forces which carry with them most life-giving power are economized and preserved from waste. The value of things cannot be measured by length of years. When at the touch of a hand, the glance of an eye, the tone of a voice, suddenly the great ocean of life wells up within us and, lost in one wild moment, self and not-self, subject and object, Man and Nature become one — such a moment, such an ecstasy is worth a lifetime of mere negation.

Man demands ecstasies of life. Without these he is unsatisfied. Nature, however, does not exist in order to satisfy this want; very rarely does she go about to satisfy it. This is one witness that no Optimistic Theory can answer. In view of this thirst for ecstasy which Nature is not destined to satisfy Moralists and Optimists, in fact, seem as those who offer wine and oil to one who has lost his love. And remembering our criterion of happiness, that it should imply abandonment, annihilation of time, extermination of past and future, oblivion to all but the present — that it should be a madness, an ecstasy — we have a right to ask, do these pallid theories of Duty and Renunciation, of the Worship of Streams of Tendency and female statues of the Genius of Humanity answer what we need? Does the pouring out of the cup of life untasted, does the putting away of the flowers of life unplucked that we may bind future generations also to this Ghost, this Phantom, this Shadow, this Illusive Ideal, this Ideal Illusion benefit them or us? In a little while we shall be dead and forgotten. In a little they also will be dead and forgotten — let us therefore turn from the Ideal to the Real, from Death to Life.

Non mortui laudabunt te, Domine; neque omnes qui descendunt in infernum. Sed nos, qui vivimus benedicimus Domino ex hoc nunc et usque in saeculum!

To withdraw contemptuously away from metaphysic however on the ground that it deals with abstraction and revolves in a circle is not wise — a nearer contemplation reveals the fact that the latest and most elaborate metaphysical systems do nothing more than reaffirm with scientific exactness what all men necessarily believe. Identity of subject and object — the universality of the idea that goes out of itself in order to return to itself more completely. These are but elaborate and technical ways of expressing the fact which every human being recognizes, that we are born into a world in which we find ourselves the microcosm. There is the mind, there is what the mind perceives and there is the unity between what it perceives and what it is. Hegelianism is at its weakest, we are told, when it attempts to deal with 'external Nature' and we can well believe it — this 'external Nature' takes a malicious, an incorrigible pleasure in reducing premature syntheses to their right proportion. But there is no necessity for alarm — though transitory, as all philosophical systems are, Hegel's system serves the present generation well enough in its attempt to find metaphysical justification for the New Paganism. If the spirit is everything and the idea is found most fully when it realizes the difference between subject and object only to transcend them both — then it is quite legitimate to put the chief stress upon the second of these two factors. What we call Nature is as necessary to mind as Mind is to Nature and we have a right as far as action is concerned to put the emphasis where we please. The wheel has come full circle and philosophy once more proves herself the politest of doorkeepers. Where metaphysic gives way under the blows of a Materialism that, it must be admitted, has limitations of its own is with regard to its presumptuous axiom that the satisfaction of personal desire is unable to afford the pleasure which can be reached by abstracting from personal desire all that is personal. It cannot be retorted too often that what really gives pleasure is the accentuation, not the diminution, of personality, and that in the composition of personality the passions must ever play the principle part.

This Christianity has seen, this philosophy has refused to see. How long must we call upon the proud spiritual thinkers to recognize what every child and illiterate person recognizes already, that the most real thing in the world is the keen sudden impact of the mind, through the senses, upon a concrete object of external Nature? This is the beginning and end of Life! This is the beginning and end of Love! This is what remains when all the philosophical explanations that have tried to explain this away have been explained away themselves.

Science, theology, metaphysics, all have this evil, that they tend by analysis, by premature explanation or by abstraction to remove from our minds that sense of the mystery and fullness and richness of life which is the beginning and the end of wisdom. The passions have the opposite effect to this — they may burn and blight, they may bruise and break, they may lead to tragedy and despair, but at any rate those who have served them know what they have served: when the end comes they may be thankful to see it. They die, but —*vixerunt*— they have at least lived.

NOTE ON THE TEXT

The manuscript of this essay is held in the extensive Powys collection of Syracuse University. It is fifty pages long and on the front cover bears the inscription 'Written about 1910'. Whether this inscription is in the hand of John Cowper Powys or of Phyllis Playter is unclear, but it is known that Miss Playter dated a number of Powys's early manuscripts, presumably in consultation with the author, when they changed hands.

COMMENTARY

'The New Paganism' has much in common with Powys's contemporary study *John Keats: or Popular Paganism* (sections of which were published by Cecil Woolf in 1993), although the essay lacks some of the high-spirited, almost knock-about rumbustiousness with which Powys chose to fling open that book in the 'Dedicatory Epistle' to Aunt Betsy Plantagenet. Essentially, both works proclaim the same message.

We may now be inclined to regard Powys's attitude towards the working-classes, and particularly towards working-class prostitutes as naïvely romantic, something which could only be the product of an upper-middle-class male sensibility, but there can be no doubt that it was genuinely held. Powys may have ignored the sheer, grinding poverty which drove such women onto the streets and the violence to which they were subject (although he tackles this in 'The Entermores') in order to focus upon their experience of 'the primal creative ecstasy' — but we cannot, in fairness, retrospectively condemn an author for belonging to the gender, class and period into which he was born. Powys certainly shared his brother Llewelyn's view that the social conventions of their class were an 'enormous wire trap' and he was desperate to escape them. He found that escape in the company of street girls such as the now famous Lily, as well as with Tom Jones (who had initiated Powys into the 'philosophy' of Keats) and 'his girls'.

What will also be clear from this essay is that Powys's later philosophical works such as *The Art of Happiness* and *In Defence of Sensuality* have their origins very early in his career and stem from his notion of New, or Popular, Paganism, especially in such statements as:

> It cannot be retorted too often that what really gives pleasure is the accentuation, not the diminution, of personality, and that in the composition of personality the passions must ever play the principle part.

From a biographical point of view, it is interesting to note that Powys's well-known flirtation with Catholicism seems, both here and in 'The Entermores', to be waning while his condemnation of his father's Church is as vehement as ever. It may be that Catholicism, or Anglo-Catholicism, had begun to lose its attraction a few years earlier than the composition of this essay, as the personality of his brother-in-law Harry Lyon lost some of its magnetism for Powys and Harry drew his sister Margaret ever more deeply into the Church. This however, is pure speculation on my part and, as Powys says, 'All speculative thought is of the nature of Negation.'

'The New Paganism' is part of a growing body of work, now being discovered and brought into print, from that hitherto empty period in Powys's literary career between the publication of *Poems* in 1899 and *The War and Culture* in 1914. These include his essay on 'G. K. Chesterton' (published in *The Powys Journal* iii, 1993), his unfinished novel 'Owen Prince' (*The Powys Journal* iv, 1994) and 'The Entermores', and are important not only because they form a body of work which is coherent thematically and stylistically, but also because they throw a new and revealing light on Powys's range and development as an author. We are used to thinking of him as an author in whose works rural settings provide the background for the interaction between characters who are, in the main, contemplative and introspective. They are works, with the notable exception of his grand crowd and battle scenes, in which thought dominates action and in which the exploration of personality as it reacts with its environment is the main focus of interest.

These newly-discovered early works reveal Powys as an author who has emerged from the aspiring laureate phase which produced his first two volumes of poetry and such works as the unpublished verse-drama 'With Love Away', but has yet to achieve the mature work for which he is most famous. Instead, we see Powys in a new and unfamiliar light Here he is urban rather than rural, with his focus clearly upon London and with the occasional, off-hand references to America one might expect of a sophisticated young man of the world. He is urbane and witty and clearly takes an almost malicious delight in exercising a cleverness quite alien to our usual image of John Cowper Powys as the 'Old Earth Man' or the Sage of Blaenau-Ffestiniog.

Above all, in these works, Powys is firmly in the public arena, addressing public themes very much in the manner of his day and in forms designed to attract a wide popular audience. The importance of the individual personality may have been his theme, but his style was very much outward-looking rather than introspective.

That he ultimately failed to make an impact in this public arena, at least as far as his written work of this period is concerned, may partly be blamed upon aspects of Powys's own character. So prodigal, it seems, was his creativity at this time that he hardly seems to have bothered about the fate of one manuscript before racing on to begin the next. The works I have referred to have all been rescued and re-assembled from sometimes chaotic manuscript sources and it seems certain that Powys took no trouble to make fair copies or, with the exception of *Keats*, to have his work typed and presented to publishers.

It could also have been the failure of this early, public, work to make an impact, together with the increasing amount of time he spent in America, away from the British literary scene, that led Powys to seek a new and more individual voice. Nevertheless, 'The New Paganism' is a fascinating essay in its own right and an important addition to the Powys bibliography.

Paul Roberts

A. R. POWYS

Unemployment and the Distribution of Leisure

The common condition of unemployment is due as much to the failure to distribute leisure as to the failure to distribute work; yet to consider the question from the first point of view appears to present less difficulty in finding a solution to the problem than does the approach to it through the wish to give all their share of work.

The following paragraphs ask whether the means suggested in them would not provide as well for a proper division of work among the people of England as for a proper distribution of leisure

No suggestion is made below of a way to increase trade and so also to increase work; neither is there here any proposal about the movement of unemployed persons from areas where there is no work to areas where there is, or will be, work. It may be that if the suggestions made as a question below are accepted by those who know that trade would improve a little and in this case it is probable that the population in areas where there is little or no work would gradually move to areas where leisure and work would be more evenly allotted. This difficulty of giving a very stationary population mobility is separate from the question raised here; it is, however, closely associated with a very different matter — that is — 'housing' and the cost of housing; and it points to the adoption of less permanent dwellings, dwellings that can be quickly built on new sites and quickly removed from those sites without spoiling them for other uses, even for uses connected with agriculture. The way to deal with the immobility of certain masses of the unemployed is another matter than that which is the subject of these paragraphs. Reference is made to it here to indicate that for a time it is a thing that may hinder the full development of the advantages otherwise to be gained from the adoption of the proposals made here.

The question, then, that is asked here is the following.

Would not the evil of the terribly wrong distribution of leisure, and consequently of the terribly wrong distribution of employment in England, be largely lessened by the passage by an Act of Parliament regulating the number of working days in the week so as to make them equal to the number of man-hours needed for the work available or to be done in the year?

Or, to ask the question a little differently, would not this evil be ended or very nearly ended were England to accept a six- or a five-day week, perhaps as follows: Sunday, Monday, Tuesday, Wednesday, Saturday?

Having asked this question, almost with the optimistic conviction of the White Knight of *Alice in Wonderland*, who so happily invented many ingenious devices never for a moment seeing those single flaws in them which rendered his care valueless, and before going into details which may possibly save the advocate of this proposal from the good-humoured — almost affectionate — reception we have all given to this dear crazy horseman, I desire to refer to two facts in our way of life to-day and to their origin.

Mr. Willett and the War made us, and the whole clock-served world, accept his daylight-saving trick. This had been of immense benefit to man; but it could never have been accepted had not mankind come habitually to rely on the clock face for his time. *The success of this scheme rests on the confirmed use of an artificial habit.* Willett recognised and made use of this habit, and man agreed to hoodwink himself, and since then has happily done so with his eyes open.

The second fact to which I refer is the firm tradition of man in England, and in all Christendom, to keep Sunday a day of leisure, a workless day — a day of rest: and of more recent years, almost within the memory of the majority of older men, to this seventh day of rest has been added the half of a sixth day.

Of what immediately is to follow I would ask [those] who believe that the Biblical Commandments are divine to read with patience and thought; for though it may at first seem to these people that I write blasphemy, I think it is not so; if it is, I am deceived.

When Moses gave commandments to the tribes he led, he gave

A. R. Powys in Norway, c.1925.

them to a world which knew not machinery. The Day of rest that was ordered through him to be observed, has been noted again and again by Christian and infidel philosophers precisely to accord with the needs of man in those days while yet he had not mastered the use of steam or gained control of other reservoirs of power. Automatically as the nineteenth century passed, the half day added to the Mosaic twenty-four hours of rest, together with two other circumstances, touched on below, helped to make the division of leisure and of labour more equitable in England. These additional safeguards from an unhappy unemployment were prescribed by no Moses and by no Prophet. Guided by a silent revelation, or, if the reader prefers the phrase, by the evolving forces of human life, Man in England was not burdened through that increasing mechanical century by more than a normal quality of unemployment.

One of the two other causes of this partly artificial condition in England was the fact that within the sea-washed beaches of her shores she did more than her share of the world's work, she produced great quantities of the goods needed by all the other races, so the workday hours were filled with full employment for nearly all her sons. Every child is to-day taught in school the reason why this artificial good fortune overtook her and every thoughtful man would be incredulous were he told that England would take so large a part of the world's manufactures. That source of employment is ended, or nearly ended. Today we have more nearly returned to a position of equality among the manufacturing nations. In the ordinary course of affairs it is likely that we will eventually do no more of the world's work than may be said to be our normal share. This means that in an increasingly mechanical age we shall have more of this terrifying leisure to spare. But does not leisure lose its terror and become desirable when it is more or less evenly distributed among the men and women of a people? The real cause, then, of the great increase in leisure to-day is the very rapid development of machinery. I have not attempted to estimate the number of hours of leisure whch machines have given us, I leave such precise statements to the statistician; it is sufficient for me that my eyes have seen great buildings raised in nine months where no buildings stood and this with half, or less than half, the expenditure of the labour that would have been used but thirty years ago. The amount of work to be done in England increases much less rapidly than does the mechanical means whereby it is done. The consequence is that we now have the increased leisure our best economists have led us to hope the blessed machines would give us. They have told us that the machine would give us this leisure and it has done so. The abnormal prosperity of England in the nineteenth century disguised this fact from us; the prayed-for leisure is suddenly come upon us. We have it but instead of buying happiness it has made [a] million men and women miserably wretched.

The Mosaic law, by ordering every seventh day to be a day of rest, prevented unemployment in the old days and gave man a then proper proportion of leisure. If we recognise the wonderful skill resting in this artificial device — many still believe it had its origin in God — we would learn from it how to divide our leisure to-day and we would order that every sixth or even every fifth day should be a day of rest. In a year we would have, instead of fifty-two leisured weekends, either 61 or 73 according as might be found desirable by calculation or by practice.

I would then very seriously ask those who have thought long of this matter if it is not proper, if it is not our duty, so to order our weekdays? And in case this plan may be given consideration at all let us here record factors that would help it to succeed: namely the existence of a proper and strong respect for the day of rest may be used.

In England, and indeed throughout Christendom, the respect for Sunday as a day of rest is far older and far stronger that ever is, or was, the regard for the clock's face as arbiter of time. But it is on this strong regard that Willett built the success of his scheme. Surely then it will be wise to make use of as powerful an obedience to custom and multiply the Sundays in the year until the week's workdays are related to the work that is to be done in the week.

And those who have concerned themselves with this question of unemployment have sought by one device or another to divide the work that is to be done evenly among those that are there to do it. They have sought by arranging for men to work less than full time or less than the full number of weekdays and by other ways to reach this desirable end. But such rules will not be accepted by man any more than would have been an order that he should rise at seven instead of at eight. The Daylight Saving Act works because a single trick was willingly accepted, because an established and strong tradition was used in a new way for man's good. Is it not wise to learn from this, and using the respect in which we bear a workless Sunday, to free man from the inconvenience and suffering he may endure from the sore ill called unemployment?

Already the Trade Unions have created the machinery to enforce the custom of resting on Sunday by their rule which orders special rates of pay for work on that day and on Saturday afternoon. Whilst these continue in force the rest day can be secured.

If it is agreed that in principle it is not wrong to shorten the week in this way and therefore [not] a thing that must on no account be done, it will be admitted that a considerable reduction in unemployment is bound to follow the adoption of this proposal. But the proposal must not be accepted even in theory without a consideration of the other effects so great a change would have on our lives. Let us see what effect this change would have on the standard of living, on the wages of the workmen, and on the wage bills of the employer.

It appears to the author of this scheme that wages should be paid weekly as at present and that they should at the end of the year amount to the same sum in £ *s.d.* as they do at present. In a word the weekly wage would have the same relation to each day of a man's life as it does now.

If this presumption is accepted it would follow that the employer's wage bill would be greater than it is now by nearly the whole sum that would be paid were the present unemployed in work. And this presumption is based on an assumption that the amount of work to be done in England remains constant. One result of this total increase in wages would be a fall in the purchasing power of the pound by perhaps as much as 2/6, but more probably a less sum. A trained economist would no doubt be able to foretell the exact difference in this respect.

One consequence of this change can be foretold. The dole tax would no longer be necessary, its place would be taken by the payment of real wages. The domestic budget of the employing and professional classes would be little changed, for what is gained by the saving of the dole tax would be spent in increased wages and in slightly increased living costs.

The general standard of living of the working classes would remain *on the average* the same as they are now, that is to say the standard of those now employed would be a little reduced while the standard of those now unemployed would be considerably improved.

The sacrifices to be made by those who are better off than the dole-paid and the quite unpaid would, I believe, be willingly borne in the interests of the last-named class and perhaps by the patriot and the humane in the interests of the nation or of suffering fellow men. The self-respect of the out-of-work would gradually be restored along with his physical well-being.

In no case would any man feel dependent on the charity of his neighbours or the state, for the work that is to be done could not be done except all or nearly all were employed.

Leaving the money side of the question that has been raised here, it is well to consider how this increase in the number of workless weekends would affect the relationship of this nation with the other nations which still adhered to the seven-days week. Doubtless there would be inconvenience, particularly at the ports and in regard to postal arrangements and communications. It is held, however, that these difficulties and inconveniences would be more than met by the advantages which accrue to the nation. Neither in the business world would these inconveniences appear very serious, for is it not already a fact that for no short five minutes do the hours of the London Stock Exchange overlap with those of New York? And do the great ships already, unless they are out of commission, load and unload at the weekend when they are in English ports and this in spite of the increased wages of those who serve the docks?

It may be said too, by some who first read these paragraphs, that other nations in other times have tried a change in the number of days of the week. The French did it at the time of the Rebellion [*sic*] but they did so from abstract theory unrelated to real life and merely out of a love for, or worship of, the decimal system. It is said that the Russians use a five-day week to-day. If this is so, and if the account of that country and its condition is at all truly represented by the English newspapers and returning tourist, it appears that this change also is made without relationship to real life and for no other than a religious reason, namely, to assert the supremacy of the State in the face of the Orthodox Church.

Finally, in an England of conservative socialists and socialist conservatives, the advocate of this scheme fears most the conservative element of this people; for will not the instinct of all men be to ejaculate 'impossible — fantastic — impracticable' or like words and turn the question aside without considering what answer is the true one. The sorrow of the unemployed is real, in making answer let that be remembered, that sorrow must not be continued by obstinate desire to uphold an age-long custom. And it should be most emphatically remembered that the age-long custom of the seventh day of rest by practice has been shown to fulfil man's needs. It is the fulfilment of his needs that the true conservative should uphold, be he of the red or of the blue party, and it is not the accident that a seventh rest day has been suitable.

'Alice' and Unemployment

SIR,—You are no coward; will you take this risk of publishing a letter that may be as crazy as at first sight it looks? Unemployment can be cured in one week by Act of Parliament, thus: "Be it enacted that from now on the week shall have five days: Sunday, Monday, Tuesday, Wednesday and Saturday."

This done, the working days in the year would be decreased in proportion to the number of unemployed, and the workless folk would immediately work. Maybe money values would fall equally; but our monetary position would remain as it now is, with one difference. Taxes for the dole would cease and the money thus saved would buy just that which we now can buy with our incomes. The difference would be that the stamina of the nation would be maintained, because all would have work, and leisure, so badly distributed now, would be equally divided among the people.

A. R. POWYS

20 Buckingham Street, Strand, W.C.2

NOTE ON THE TEXT

The typescript of this article is part of a collection of A. R. Powys's papers which I was given by his younger daughter, Eleanor Walton. It has no title. There is no sign that it has ever been printed; this is perhaps not surprising, as it deals with a subject which was not, of course, within ARP's professional field as an architect, but clearly it reflects his awareness of social problems.

That ARP had socialist leanings at a much earlier date, when he had his first married home in Battersea in London, we can learn from a letter written by his mother Mary Cowper Powys to Theodore Powys on 27 January 1910: 'Bertie will vote for Mr. John Burns, I am glad of that, for he is a good man.' (*The Powys Society Newsletter* 40, 14.) John Burns was a socialist and a radical of considerable influence; he was the Battersea representative in Parliament and on the London County Council in the 1890s and early 1900s. MCP's comment is interesting also for its indication of her own awareness of the London political scene as seen from her rural and ecclesiastical Somerset situation.

The paper can be approximately dated by the references to 'Mr. Willett' and the Daylight Saving Act and to the Russian five-day week. William Willett was a Chelsea builder (1865–1915) who advocated setting forward the clocks in spring and summer, but little enthusiasm was shown for the idea until the Germans adopted it in March 1916, followed by the British; it lapsed in peacetime, but the principle was revived in 1922 and continues to this day.

Daylight-saving required an Act of Parliament, which ARP would have liked for his much more radical suggestion of a week of five days. Such a week of five days was in fact introduced in the Soviet Union in 1929, and superseded in 1931 by a six-day week, itself abandoned in 1940. It seems that the letter printed in *Week-End Review* for 4 March 1933 (reproduced on the previous page) marks exactly the period in which he wrote the article.

Stephen Powys Marks

Stephen Reynolds 'in frighting gear' on Sidmouth beach in August 1909, a month after the first meeting with Katie.
(photograph by courtesy of Christopher Scoble)

* *Best let Reynolds explain. 'Frights are two-legged fish. When a lady who is walking down to a boat with the intention of hiring it hears one fisherman call out to another: 'Dick, there's a fright for thee there!' she is apt to look a little startled. It has to be explained to her that* fright *is a way of pronouncing* freight. *But I don't think most ladies like it, after that.'*

CHRISTOPHER SCOBLE

Katie Powys and Stephen Reynolds
A Passion Foredoomed

Stephen Reynolds was born in Devizes in 1881, the son of a local businessman. After school and university, he went to Paris to teach himself to write, but his stories would not sell and, on return to England in 1903, he suffered a nervous breakdown which nearly killed him. In the convalescent years which followed he wrote his only novel, The Holy Mountain. *Through Edward Garnett he was introduced to literary London and established close and lasting friendships with Edward Thomas and Joseph Conrad.*

In 1906, his annus mirabilis, *there came a unique experience which was to shape the whole course of his life. On a brief holiday in Sidmouth, he fell in love with a fisherman's family with whom he was staying. He abandoned all middle class allegiance to live with them for the rest of his life. In 1908 he published* A Poor Man's House, *painting life in a working-class family from the inside. It shot him to overnight fame. By the summer of 1909, the young stocky figure on Sidmouth beach had become an established tourist attraction. Those who had read the book, now wanted to meet the man.*

[*This article is formed of extracts from Christopher Scoble's book,* Fisherman's Friend: a life of Stephen Reynolds, *to be published in November 2000 by Halsgrove, Tiverton, Devon.*]

The frighting season (*see note* below photograph*) at Sidmouth started early that summer and by the middle of May Reynolds was already rushed off his feet.[1] For some reason there were more people around seeking trips out with the young stocky figure on Western beach — and many of them were women. No longer were they surprised to discover the man on the oars was a writer; they had already read the book.

On 18 June a small party of tourists arrived from the village of Montacute in Somerset.[2] It consisted of the vicar, the Reverend Charles Francis Powys, his wife and three of their daughters, Marian (May), Lucy, and Philippa — known to the family as Katie. Altogether, there were ten surviving children in the family of whom the greatest noise was to be made in the world by the distinguished literary triumvirate — John Cowper, Theodore and Llewelyn. For Katie too writing was an essential of everyday life. She was to publish a novel, and write several others, but her sensitive and expressive nature made her above all a poet — as Theodore once said 'the only poet of our family'.[3]

Of the daughters she had the most marked of the Powys physical characteristics — large-boned with rather heavy features, intense eyes and a generous smile. She was a handsome, awkward girl, impetuous, strong-willed with an adventurous mind thirsting for knowledge. The last child but two, she was now 23 and had lived for most of her life in the enclosed atmosphere of the west country vicarage, dreaming of the world and of becoming a writer. Though surrounded by such a large family, she was introspective, nervous, mystical. In adolescence she grew closest to her younger sister Lucy, a shy and gentle child, to whom she acted as guide and protector. The two girls planned when they were older to run a farm together.

They had discovered Sidmouth on a holiday in February of the previous year when Reynolds was living with Hueffer in London — and it had proved a revelation. Even in the wintry weather, they had climbed the cliffs around the town, explored the woods on High Peak, delighted in the little esplanade and the closeness of the sea.[4] It was for both their first escape into a wider world, and the chance to meet new people. They determined to come back. This second holiday in June 1909 was to change the whole course of Katie's life. She met Reynolds and fell instantly in love, a love that was to survive unblemished until her death as an old woman more than fifty years later.

On this summer visit they spent more time on the beach, swimming, watching the fishing activity all around, going for the occasional row with Katie at the oars. They met Bob and Tom.* In the

* *Bob Woolley, with whom Reynolds lived. Tom was his brother.*

evenings after dinner they would walk the Esplanade, watching the sea and the other summer visitors. The previous year they had come in contact with Melville Mackay, the Sidmouth photographer who had helped with the publicity for *A Poor Man's House* and was to contribute the photographs for *Alongshore*. On this occasion he lent Katie a copy of the book that all Sidmouth was talking about,[5] which she devoured avidly in her bed in the half-light of the summer mornings. It had a powerful effect. 'The more I read, the more I became aware of a new self. ... It sang to me of the beauty of form and of colour, of the mystery of thought and of emotion.'[6]

And then she bumped into Reynolds himself — or rather into Margot,* the usual source of all Reynolds' first introductions. As someone who wanted herself so badly to write, she was knocked out by this meeting with a real live author and by watching the book and its characters unfolding before her eyes. At the beginning of July she confided to her diary: 'It does attract me to read a book whose characters move and speak separate from the book in front of me. It gives me also a keen pleasure to have to do with the writer though Lucy spoke first to him before we knew we were in trouble with his dog'.[7]

When she met him on the beach below the Bedford Steps, she was breathless and embarrassed. 'I came to give him praise. I came to give him thanks. But in my nervousness my words tumbled forth and my expressions were of the foolish.' She invested this first meeting with a deep emotional power.

> Together upon the shore we stood; indifferent to the people passing above, as souls banished, but now joined, we stood. Singly, but together, with an understanding and a sympathy more mysterious than the laying on of hands; more occult than the crossing of stars. The falling of the water was

* *Reynolds' brindled Great Dane, almost as tall as him, who could knock people down in the first excited encounter. 'Everywhere they said, 'shouldn't like to meet he in the dead o' night, Mister.' In stableyards they stood round watching while I washed your feet and groomed you with a borrowed dandy-brush. 'Jest like a bloomin' hoss,' they said.'*

Katie Powys and Bob Woolley, Reynolds' fisherman friend, at Sidmouth in October 1929, just after the writing of 'Phoenix'.
(photograph by courtesy of Christopher Scoble)

> forgotten, the powerful burning of the sun was unheeded. I was affrighted; I turned and I fled. As a stranger I had sought him and he had not rebuked me. I had spoken and he had heard. Up the steps I hurried. From the welcome of the others I hid my head, so fervent was the meaning of my secret, so significant the crowning of my love.[8]

By the last week of their holiday, Katie and Lucy were spending more and more time on the beach — 'We walk but little now, the characters are too interesting' .[9] They gave nicknames to some of the new friends they met, but Katie had a special private one for Reynolds in her diary — Olaf, an obscure reference perhaps to the daring medieval King and patron saint of Norway. The diary entries were taking on an intimacy of their own: 'He must forgive me for calling him by that name but as he assumes a character I must put an assumed name to him. With that I can speak of him more freely'.[10]

As she fell for the first time deeply in love, he was her release.

> Here was one who broke all paltry conventions. In contemplating his book and perceiving his ways, I unearthed his codes and they incited me. They were of the infinite and of the groundswell. ... Below the steps of the sea-wall, below the passing to and fro of the indifferent, I questioned him, and he answered. There, at the slow turning of the day, he disclosed to me the purport of literature. I remembered his words and garnered them in the recesses of my heart. Close by his side, upon the pebbles we talked, and my love for him shivered and blossomed.[11]

On 9 July, the last full day of their holiday, Katie went out for a row with Tom and surprisingly broke through the usual barrier of reserve. 'The sea broke our shyness and I felt as I talked with him we might have known each other as Father and I do now ...' That evening a blustering rain came on and she gave Reynolds a hand in dragging the boats up the beach above high water mark. He was becoming used to the admiration of lady frights, but by now he must have known that this was no ordinary summer visitor. That evening, as a parting gesture, he signed his name in both Katie's and Lucy's birthday books. And Katie wrote in her diary a farewell phrase that could have come straight from Reynolds' pen 'We go tomorrow. The sea wails ...'[12] She was already beginning to sink her identity in his.

The departure from Sidmouth that Saturday morning was made easier because Reynolds was himself going up to London, armed with the proofs of the *Mountain* to read on the way, to meet Jewett, Lane's American manager, and discuss publication of his books in the States.[13] He offered to accompany the two sisters by train as far as Yeovil. After lunch that day Katie carried the precious copy of *A Poor Man's House* down to where Mackay lived but, finding him out, followed on down the Gut to Bob's cottage and left it with him to return. There she met Reynolds himself and had a brief chat, wishing all the time that she might stay longer. He went with them as promised the first leg of the journey and the parting for Katie was especially poignant: 'my last word and last look was on the platform of the Junction and he disappeared entirely at Yeovil with his proofs'.[14]

The picture was to remain in her mind and he in her thoughts continuously throughout the coming weeks, growing stronger as reality faded into fantasy. A week later, on return from an evening excursion to Weston super Mare, he was still at the forefront of her mind: 'Coming back so late at night was something quite new. I wished for an apparition of Olaf but Sidmouth or Devizes successfully hid him ...'[15] It was an image and a longing that was not going to go away. For someone so romantic and impressionable, from a wholly sheltered background, there was nothing for it but surrender to this first overwhelming experience of love. But she had made for any woman a fatal mistake — fallen in love with a homosexual man without the least suspicion of the barrier that stood between them. It could only end in disaster.

[*Reynolds published his novel* The Holy Mountain *that September to a very mixed reception. By the summer of 1910 he was putting the finishing touches to his third book,* Alongshore. *Katie came down again this year, but just for one day.*]

On Saturday 28 May, Katie Powys arrived once more at Sidmouth station — for just a day trip this year, again with her younger sister Lucy. Her life was about to change for Lucy had started to court a husband and the old plans of working a farm together were quietly disintegrating. Much of the excitement of the previous holiday had burnt off in the ensuing twelve months, but she knew whom she was looking out for.

> As we went down the front we felt sad for there seemed nothing but strangers till I saw Tom Woolley on the beach and better still Olaf sitting on the edge of a boat. He recognized us and after dinner I ventured to speak to Tom. Then I asked Bob to let me go for a row, they settled on Olaf to take me, so Bob launched us on the sea ...[16]

They were alone together once more. The sea was a little rough, but she did not notice. They talked. She asked him what he thought of Walt Whitman, her favourite poet, and they both agreed he was a fine writer. They talked about Socialism and much to her disappointment he told her of his ambivalence: 'I wish he was an entire one but he says he favours them where he can't stand the Conservatives and Liberals'.[17] For Katie, this was the first man outside the family circle to whom she could speak freely of politics, religion and literature and who, though hired with the boat, would listen to her views with genuine attention and treat her as an equal. These few minutes out to sea now entirely rekindled the urgent feelings of the previous summer. 'It was over too quick but it gave Sidmouth its old delightful appearance. The leaving was cruel.' [18]

Reynolds, highly sensitive to sexual situations, could have been in little doubt about the nature of her feelings. When confronted with vulnerability, his kindliest instincts were aroused. Yet, at the same time, he hid his embarrassment behind an urgent smoke-screen of friendly gestures. Once again he was at his most courteous, helped the girls sort out their return train and gave Katie the postcard of a yacht taken by Melville Mackay, who, he told her, had also provided some splendid photos for his new book (she caught the title as 'Along the Shore') which was coming out that autumn.[19] Katie, who could not guess at his dark secret, took these friendly attentions at face value.

They meant a lot. She travelled back to Montacute that evening, clutching the postcard, recalling every word he had spoken on the boat, and thinking of the book that was to come. Here at least was some consolation for the desertion of Lucy.

[*The following summer of 1911 was a scorcher, the hottest in England since 1868. Reynolds spent much of it bathing naked on the men's beach of West Bay. He had given over the much-reviled occupation of frighting to Bob and Tom, though he made an exception for some special visitors. He was writing a series of articles for the* Westminster Gazette, *entitled 'Weekends at Nesscombe', rather similar in style and content to Gissing's* Ryecroft. *For one of them that July he wrote up an incident in which he had led the fishermen in the cliff rescue of a visitor from Wiltshire. They had saved his life.*]

Katie Powys in Somerset had heard of the cliff rescue from her family; but tantalisingly they had determined not to send her a copy of the report in the local paper, for fear of untoward consequences. She noted in her diary: 'I have just had an excellent letter from Stephen Reynolds and since then he has been saving folks from the Cliff, in fact High Peak. An account of it was in the Western Gazette and both Lucy and Violet* dare not lend it to me'.[20]

This may have been purely paranoia, but is one intimation of the new intensity of Katie's feelings towards Reynolds since the last day visit to Sidmouth the previous summer. Her reclusive existence in the country and perhaps too her decision to start serious writing was already affecting her heightened sensitivity. On a visit to relatives in London in February 1910 she had had the first in a series of panic attacks. Left on her own one evening 'I got rather nervous ... I felt as if some horrible demon was on the point of attacking.' It was a major relief to hear the doorbell and her friends return.[21] The family, rather naïvely, put it down to over-excitement brought on by the story she was writing;[22] but it was an ominous forewarning of things to come.

It was about this time in 1910 that Katie and Lucy had gone to help their brother Will on his farm at Witcombe, near Montacute. There they worked happily tending the cows and learning the hidden secrets

* *Theodore's wife.*

of cheesemaking, training for the farm they were planning to run together themselves. The major shock for Katie in the spring of 1911 was Lucy's marriage and the sudden rupture of such a close bond. When Lucy left Montacute to live with her husband in Hampshire, Katie was left stranded with her life plans in ruins.

Scarcely surprising then that she should turn emotionally and with revived energy to her old fantasy. In May she took her courage in both hands and wrote direct to Reynolds in Sidmouth. Ostensibly, it was to ask how everybody was and when his next books were coming out. But she also dropped a tentative invitation, as to a one-time farmer, to come and visit her at Witcombe and see the farm for himself. He was quick to head off the approach.

> Thank you for your letter and kind invitation to call. But unfortunately I never seem to get anywhere except full speed up and down the line. I've got a sister and sundry nieces living near Bournemouth whom I haven't succeeded in seeing for three years! Now we have a motor boat which only myself can run I am more tied than ever.[23]

But Dot and her children on the farm at Parkstone, and the time-consuming *Puffin* on the beach, were only the flimsiest of excuses.

For Katie, however, the remainder of the letter, chatty though somewhat distant, was the beginning of a correspondence. It was the 'excellent' letter recorded in her diary. It provided the excuse to write again. If the family wanted to keep her away from the *Western Gazette*, it can only have been because they sensed the new disturbance to her equilibrium.

Lucy came down to Montacute for August bank holiday and that week the two sisters made their annual day's pilgrimage to Sidmouth, as if life were back to normal again. Katie had alerted Reynolds to their arrival and had brought him a duck from the farm ready for cooking.[24]

Once again, they searched for him on the beach but saw only Bob and Tom. They were told he was up in his study, and Katie set off on her own to find him, for the first time at home in his lair.

> How my knees gave and how with loud beating my heart rose

> to my ears when they told me my love was still with them and we should see him in the upper room. In a room laden with books, in a room with an opening towards the sea, he stretched forth his right hand. My spirit leapt as a playing deer, leapt with inspired awe, for through the entrance of his sanctuary I had come, into his very presence I was admitted. Before, it was to see him, now it was to know him.
>
> Strange and various were the intimations he threw out to me ... In love I beheld him. I felt his range of vision was boundless. Merciless he could be. Hypocrisy was his abomination and deceit ran from him. He spared no man. To revenge injustice he would face the stake. Men feared him. Children knew him as one of themselves, they forsook their games to follow him.[25]

He promised to take her out for a row once again that afternoon. 'With intense happiness I left him, with unbounded joy I found my sister.'[26] The two sisters went for a swim and talked on the Esplanade with Uncle Sam.* They took a stroll a little way up both Peak and Salcombe Hills, returning hungry for lunch in Fore Street.[27] 'My heart it would not rest, so tremulous it was within me.'[28]

That afternoon she waited for him below the Bedford Steps.

> The fishermen steadied the boat, and the oars lay cross-wise as he came lightly running down the steps and down the beach. Their calls rang fresh within my ears as they slid her towards the sea; and more pleasant than a thousand sheep bells was the grating of her keel as she parted the shingle. They signed me to get in, the light waves lifted the bow of the boat. They floated her off, he sprang with his knee upon her side. He caught up the oar. He steered her forth. The aged fisherman smiled, and stepped back from the touch of the waves. He lifted his hand as if he blessed us.
>
> My heart flooded, and the veils of my happiness were loosed. One short moment of time I would now share with

* *Sam Woolley, the uncle of Bob and Tom, and popular hero of* A Poor Man's House.

> him whom I loved. One passing hour we were to be alone in a narrow wooden craft. There to possess him. His eyes searched mine, searched and pinioned me forever. In the wilderness of his sight I was lost.[29]

Reynolds was keen to keep the atmosphere low-key. He told her all his mundane woes, how swamped he was with work, both fishing and writing.[30] Katie missed most of it. 'In the midst of so much, words fell to be forgotten. Unmindful were my ears, but my heart it whispered tremulous heeding.'[31]

For her, it was another miraculous day — the longed-for row, tea afterwards at the Woolleys and a sudden parting with which she invested her own particular superstitious significance.

> Oh I had such a nice time and I was so happy ... I did so enjoy my row. The talk was so good. I was loath to come in. He said they wanted us to have tea with them, so we did. Mrs. Woolley got it ready and I felt so hungry, but in the middle a man came and seized 'Olaf' away ... We never saw Olaf again. Still I did not mind for it made one think that not to say a 'goodbye' perhaps meant the next meeting would come sooner. I wonder.[32]

Reynolds, himself so hypersensitive to those who shared his own brand of vulnerability, was at a loss how to deal with this woman. He was the last person to be able to take her aside and talk straight. Nor was it a situation that could be circumvented by humour. He chose to be as kind and polite as he could on the surface, while maintaining a determined distance.

Soon after this latest visit, Katie wrote to him again under a literary smoke-screen, enclosing some newspaper cuttings and asking how she might get hold of some Nietzsche. He replied in strictly business fashion, kindly but like a schoolmaster addressing a rather naïve pupil: 'Nietzsche is published in a cheap edition by Foulis of Edinburgh. Book shops can get him. *Thus Spake Zarathustra* is his celebrated work, but I think *Beyond Good and Evil* is about the best of his books for a peck at. He's good as an antidote against sloppy sentimentalism, but not good to read as an authority on things, because he is a special pleader for comparatively few philosophical ideas. Therefore, read, mark, learn, but don't inwardly digest too much of him'.[33]

This was a lecture designed to keep the relationship at arm's length, but the reading plan, with its call to action and involvement, had just the opposite effect. By the same token, the signature to the letter, intended to appear cheery and offhand, might be read quite differently by someone in love: 'I hope yourself and the cows and the cheeses are flourishing'.[34]

[*Reynolds' book of political articles,* Seems So! A Working-Class View of Politics, *written jointly with Bob and Tom Woolley, came out that November and struck an immediate chord with political analysts and the reading public, puzzling over the increasingly violent wave of industrial unrest which it set out to explain. It was his best selling book since* A Poor Man's House. *But that autumn he was increasingly sucked in to fisheries politics in London, a process that was eventually to put paid to his writing life. When Katie returned to Sidmouth in the summer of 1912, the burden of both writing and fishery affairs had brought him once more close to breaking point.*]

Since her day visit to Sidmouth the previous August, Katie Powys had kept up her correspondence with him, her only link, assuming the role of devoted pupil to his all-knowing teacher. Inspired by his example, she was sublimating her feelings in writing. By October 1911 she had completed two short stories, and was planning three more. 'One, the biggest and most deep, will be called 'The thoughts of a dairymaid' or 'While Milking' in[to] which I hope to bring in some distant time the three great things that affect humanity, that is: the elements, love and religion.' Despite the brave front, there was a growing awareness of the unequal nature of the relationship. She confided to her diary: 'I go on writing to Sidmouth and at times I have a letter from 'Olaf'; otherwise I have to content myself with different articles that come to my hand'.[35]

The short stories were not just sublimation; they were material means of attracting his attention. She sent him one in late October, just as he was setting off with Tom for France. On return on 1 November he sent her a holding reply: 'The MS. is getting itself steadily read through. When I'm finished, I'll let you know what I think; and then you'd best disbelieve me entirely! The best criticism, the only ultimate criticism, is one's own.' [36]

She was staying with her brother, Theodore, at East Chaldon when his comments on the manuscript finally arrived, the source of much pleasure. But her diary entries show how much she was measuring out her life with his letters. 'I have been to the cliffs now four times. Twice before Olaf's letters to me and twice afterward. He wrote me a splendid one on my old story, one which is full of sound advice.' [37]

In February she sent him a new manuscript, which he read on his return from London. He noted the power of feeling, always her greatest strength, but also the uneven quality of the expression.

> Your letter and sketch came while I was in Town on fishery business — rushing round furiously. The sketch, which I return, is almost grim in parts. Its faults are precisely those which I pointed out before — plenty of feeling, plenty of thought, but inattention to detail. A thing, to be artistic, must be *just so* all the way through.[38]

She was desperate to see him.

> Dreams and inward meditations were the grace of the spirit, but the flesh of the body lacked hope. To see and to hear was the repeated wish ... Written messages availed little. Words were mirages, they tempted, but they could not satisfy. My love was my irresistible want. To him I must hasten. Through mud and through heat I must reach him, through cold and through rain I must find him. Athirst with great longing I craved for him.[39]

She had been planning an earlier than usual visit to Sidmouth, but fate was against it. Still at Chaldon in December 1911, she went walking the cliffs at White Nose with her brother Llewelyn and seems to have had some presentiments of the calamity that was about to break.

That shore, how the spirit thereof has wrapped itself round me. The times Lulu and I went down before Xmas when we climbed back in the deepening darkness. Weird and strange and awe-inspiring, it shook my very soul. I felt that Olaf would have understood it. Then when the wave came towards me on the ledge, the feeling of death was not far and I wished that I could have seen him again.

... Curious how full of omens for my visit to Sidmouth [it] has been. Always something happened to prove more and more that I was not going down as I wished, and so it is.[40]

The early visit came to nothing, but the summer one went ahead as usual. In early August, she went down with Llewelyn and her elder sister Gertrude for the few days, so achingly anticipated, that were to lead to the disaster.[41] It was her fifth visit to Sidmouth, and the last she would make while Reynolds was alive.

Afterwards, back home at Witcombe, she made a tersely laconic record in her diary.

Sidmouth has come and gone.

Olaf was down there. I first saw him in the kitchen that first night. Bob took us a row the next day and we had tea at Tom's while we saw the Twins. We climbed Salcombe and High Peak. Olaf came down on us once the other side. I would go every morning down to the sea and the black lady would haunt me. Tom I met sometime. Saw Bob the first morning and Olaf never then. He came to tea on Sunday but when he left he bunked like ten thousand Aunt Marthas had been set loose after her calf. It was good to see them again. We had a lovely tea there. Bob really charming — Mrs. Woolley and the New baby. The great thing was Gertrude drawing Bob and the baby. I hated going again. I feel further away every time I go ...[42]

The diary breaks off. It was fifteen years before she would write in it again.

And it was in the late 1920s too that she felt strong enough to write *Phoenix*, the prose-poem charting her breakdown — her own version of the *Ex Profundis* book that Reynolds never wrote. In it she brought herself to face what actually had happened that August. It is a disturbing, highly emotional, but also deeply moving, account.

At the beginning there hovers the symbol of the dark lady she recorded in her diary — a woman in black by the seashore mourning another lost love — 'Only a woman with garments of mourning paced beside the white-tongued waves, steadfastly turning her eyes away from the long-limbed men'.[43]

On arrival, she combs the beach for Reynolds, but in vain.

> Where was my love? I continued my search by the high bows of the boats. I expected still to see him by the shores of the receding tides. Instead, over the waters flew the dark birds; for in the knowledge of death, the white birds hide. Lonely and disappointed, the shadow of my dawn fell before me and my spirit drooped even as a broken wing.[44]

The defining moment came on the day she walked over High Peak with Gertrude and down into the green valley below. There they are overtaken by Reynolds on his daily walk to Ladram Bay. For both parties it is a shock encounter. She stands tongue-tied before him. From her demeanour, he can tell even more clearly than before the strength of her feelings. He cannot explain to her in terms the barrier that stands between them. But on the spur of the moment, he determines on a personal declaration that should provide the hint: he is alone, loved only by the natural world around him, and so always will remain. She understands the purpose of this stark confession, but not its hidden reasoning. It is a message of devastation and despair.

> Yet another day we wandered away through the woods where in fancy the sweetest of earth-born violets grow. In heaviness I bore my heart; to see him and to hear him being my sole imperative. Onwards and onwards my sister led me; to the steep rocks where the gulls meet and have their being, to where the high cliffs stand jagged and washed to the colour of blood. Presently we returned to where the grass was greenest, to where the wind was hidden, when quicker than a meteor he

appeared. Unconscious of things mortal, unconscious of things immortal, we stood together. In mute diffidence my soul remained. Standing with his eyes searching mine I heard him cry. 'No friends but these, I have. Alone I am. None there are who love me.'

In a moment the sun turned to darkness, and the grass turned to dust. Then flashed the fiery sword from heaven, until it pierced my side. As a woman I could not speak, emboldened by love I was bound by silence. I suffered from a judgement severe. Henceforth would I know the wail of the seabirds as they gathered in the air; and my cry would follow theirs in the over-shadowed night. 'Terrible, terrible, Oh! my God! is the destruction of a woman!'

If ever mute creation desired words to confess, my spirit fast panted within me, but the ways of the world sealed my lips and the manner of man silenced my tongue. Broken and dumb as the sharp cliffs below, and as indifferent as the clouds which raced above, I remained. Passive and wrought I stood before him. I could not show the running wound to the physician himself. I dared not lift my countenance to his face. He spoke, but I could not answer. He mourned, but I could not comfort. He was sorrowful, but I dared not console. With the anguish of an imprisoned bird, my spirit beat itself against the bars of conformity. He gave; but to give to him I was denied.

Cruel are the ways of the world. Men come and men go, but how wretchedly their hands are held. The hour of their day passeth, but only the shell adorns their dwelling. In the rising of the sun there cometh rain.

Sorely stricken was my heart, and the love cords of my life were twisted in misery. There in sadness I stood apart, and in silent woe I kept his words.[45]

The remaining days were desolation. As the final day approaches, she scours the town for one last sight of him.

By hidden ways and low houses I came forth alone to where I met the sea. I paced the long stretch of the weather-beaten

> wall. All was deserted. Like the dead bellies of black horses the big boats lay where the waves could not harm them. I looked to the right, I looked to the left, but no man moved. [46]

In desperation, she goes down the Gut to Bob's cottage. In the joy of meeting Reynolds once more, she determines on a new mission for her life.

> I was afraid; unbeckoned, I sought the house where he lived. I hastened between the walls where the children play. In nervous terror I passed by the wrapped sails, where I heeded not the up-turned boat, nor the grey of sea-worn oars. At the doorway I reached out my hand. I faltered. I knocked. It was opened. I was led through the passage into the low kitchen, where before me I saw his fellow-fisherman, and the mother and babe. They rose up to receive me. With the outstretching of hands they welcomed me. When I saw them lean over the little one, the fire lighting with warm colour the figures, the cradle and the infant clothing, I understood. Astonished I could not forget the father, and the mother, and the sleeping child.
>
> They brought to my mind how in the wantonness of a tangled under-wood, the delicate primrose and the slender campion bring forth their buds in hidden secret, and their flowers in careless safety. It is there where the berries of the bramble drop sweet and unknown, for the thorns are their protection and the nettles their true defence. Here, I perceived a shelter for the lonely heart and comfort for the troubled in mind.
>
> In response to the maddened beating of my heart, my own friend appeared. My love was before us. In our midst he had come. Yea, to himself he had gathered his own, and with one accent we were glad.
>
> My soul mounted upwards. Much happiness was mine. Great joy rose as the fire before me, stretching in scarlet and gold, transforming all in its piercing heat. Through the light of its glory I beheld the one I adored. In brilliance greater than

> the day-born sun I found him. I took of his spirit, wherewith never to renounce it. Thanks-giving was the expression of my exaltation, and the magnitude of all worship was in my praise. In silent intensity I knew my affection and in the sight of him I blessed my existence. He spoke; and as at the first sound of distant breakers I caught fast my breath. Thus contentment came by the crooning of a baby and by the side of a deep-sea fisherman I foresaw my destiny. To be near my love was my satisfaction, and to live for him, my ambition.[47]

Another day, she returns to the cottage again, and waits for him in his first floor study, alone with all his books and personal possessions. He comes to her, but this time in imagination only.

> At the coming of another day, when, wrapped in my shawl, I lay in sickness of mind and body upon his couch, I was caught as if in a trance. There in the secret of his chamber, he was allowed me. There in dozing and light dreaming he touched me. Among sounds and objects he knew, I found him. He came to my side, and yet he was not. He came to the bed-pillow, and I heard him speak; I roused myself, but he was not. He approached in spirit, but not in flesh.[48]

The obsession, and the knowledge of certain loss, was too much for the delicate balance of her mind. Back at her brother Will's farm at Witcombe, she suffered, like Reynolds in 1903, a total collapse.

> Too quickly, in a moment, in a second, the mighty arm of my exaltation felled me. The waters of my want overcame me. A malady of the brain possessed me. I was sick. My passion outreached itself; the flames of my love overpowered me.[49]

She became religiously obsessed with the Cross. Very early one morning, she escaped her bedroom leaving all the pictures, books, jewellery and objects arranged in the shape of crosses. Will thought she had gone out to drown herself, and she was found and rushed back to Montacute Vicarage to the protection of her parents.[50] On 22 August, her brother, John Cowper, travelled up from his home in

Sussex to be by her side. He was sure that the stifling atmosphere of the vicarage was the real culprit: 'The real cause of all this is our present cursed system which permits no freedom to a child of unhappy and hopeless passions like Katie'.[51]

She cried out for her copy of Walt Whitman's *Leaves of Grass* which Gertrude believed was one of the causes of the trouble.[52] She would wake up in the middle of the night when her medication wore off and terrify the trained nurse put to watch over her. 'Katie becomes, just as animals do, conscious at once of anyone's fear of her, and rendered by it at once angry and bold.' [53] At three o' clock in the morning of 25 August, she got on to the window-sill of her room and threatened to throw herself out.[54] The family's thoughts turned towards institutional care.

In all of this frightening chaos, Reynolds was at the centre of her thoughts.

> I was become more and more obsessed with a vehement desire to go to my beloved. It mattered not how, as long as my face was turned to the south-west, to where lay the wide encircling bay upon which the fishermen sailed. With this one fixed idea, I bethought my will-power would suffice to induce all mankind, instantaneously to take me to his side. But in my madness I was mistaken ... I fancied my love himself was come; and that it was his footsteps I heard through the thin partition of the wall. I called, but there came no answer.[55]

So close was the identification, she began to believe that she herself was an incarnation of Reynolds and signed little notes 'Katie (S.R.)'.[56] On 27 August, John Cowper wisely decided to involve Reynolds himself. 'I have got Gertrude to write to Stephen Reynolds asking him for a letter to her commanding her to use her will to be calm. But I fear things are really beyond his power to cure.' [57]

The request came at a bad time for Reynolds. Overworked, physically ill, torn in the throes of the final conflict between his moneyless writing and the increasing burden of fisheries business, he was, as he had told George Macmillan, fast heading for his second breakdown himself. The cause of Katie's violent illness went close to the heart of his own private anxieties, and threatened to expose his own hidden secret. It was a situation on which many would have inclined to turn their backs.

He didn't. On 1 September, he drafted a careful letter, designed to calm her and give her hope for recovery. He drew on his own experience, but not so much as to waken a different kind of hope. It was a difficult tightrope to walk.

> We are all very glad to hear you are better. The great thing is, when an attack comes on, to sit tight, confident that, as it has had a beginning, so it will have an end. That practice makes perfect is even truer as regards controlling nerve-storms than it is of most things. You will find, first that they will cease to surprise you, and then that you can act in quite an ordinary manner even in the middle of them, giving no sign to anyone of your interior distress; and then, almost suddenly, you will wake up to the fact that they have ceased, only to recur at lengthening intervals, if at all. Then is the time to get thoroughly interested in some comparatively commonplace light work, so that one has, as it were, a centre to revolve round and keep one steady. As I told you before — for the relief of overstrained nature, there is nothing like a long spell of being very ordinary. And, as a matter of fact, the most original thinkers have nearly all led pretty humdrum lives themselves.
>
> Now you have begun to get better, you can go on, with constant watchfulness and care in self-management.[58]

But she was not better. The periods of remission proved something of a chimera. By the time the letter arrived, the family had decided on the safety of institutional care, and she was moved to a psychiatric home — Brislington Hall in Bristol. In one of the most ironically tragic twists of the whole story, when her father accompanied her to Bristol, she believed he was taking her to her wedding.

> My father watched from the entrance of the door. Suddenly, without a word or a prayer, he outstretched his arm to the bush of high myrtle. Heedlessly he plucked sprays of the sweet

> smelling blossoms. With dignity, he hastened down the stone-steps which divided us. Hastily, without thought, he pushed into my hands those delicate blooms — blooms of the white Myrtle — the flower of the bride.
>
> Oh! Cruel Significance. Oh! gesture fantastical!
>
> The illusion became truth. I imagined they were of a certainty taking me to my dear one. Never to be parted.
>
> The further we went, the more sure I became, and when we reached the journey's end I advanced trembling, but the church and the altar were wanting. The bridegroom was missing. Instead of the joyful pealing of bells, it was the moaning of the mad. Instead of the scattering of rice, it was the uncanny dance of the demented ... I cursed my Father and my Mother, and the day of my delivery, for here the day was turned to darkness and the night beheld no moon. I sank into the pit of madness, into the most loathsome of dungeons, there to meet the grinding of teeth and the wild tearing of hair.[59]

Amidst the despair, Reynolds' letter came as a sign of deliverance and salvation. All her personal possessions had been taken from her, but this treasure she secreted away.

> At last, at the time of the many bells, at the time of happiness and the healing of wounds, there came a message into my hands. In the depth of a cess-pool, in the tumult of feeling it was brought to me. Whether borne on the wind, I knew not; nevertheless it came in the likeness of a boat, in the shape of an high hill it appeared before me ... I caught it up in my hand, and in the tight lace of my dress I hid it. By day it revived me, by night it gladdened me. It brought the scent of spring flowers. I was better. I was happy. It revealed the One who remained by the rough waves. It renewed me as the strong smell of seaweed.[60]

It became the precious symbol of their relationship, of his care for her, and as she carried it with her around the hospital, so did she carry it through life. Held fast between the pages of her battered green volume of *Leaves of Grass*, it went wherever she did. Forty years after her death, it lies safe in that volume today.

Then, as she started to recover, a terrible recognition was borne in upon her. She had been mad, and he knew of it. He could not possibly fall in love with her now.

> How could I seek him now that the fiends of madness had hold of me? How could I go to him now that I had lain in the dung of pigs? Therefore I saw the departing of my Sun and instead the darkness of vain longing pressed heavily upon me. In the eagerness to leap the way between us, I had fallen to be seared ... I was cursed, for these arms would never encircle the head of the man I loved.
>
> Who would walk with one who smelt of the mad-house?
> Who would gather among roots blackened by fire?
> None can give birth whose dreams are a furnace,
> Whose wells are poison and whose hopes are perished.
>
> Here in my bed of affliction it was borne to me. In horror it filled my being. I gathered up my covering and wept. My tears watered the pillow even faster than the rain outside. But no one heard for there was no one to hear.[61]

Terrible as was the finality of this realisation, it was nonetheless the beginning of the healing. Here was now a rational justification for his behaviour to which she might at last come to be reconciled. Slowly over time the despair turned to hope in the fulfilment of the new determination she had made in Bob's cottage at their final meeting.

She spent years in the wilderness, working on farms more as a penitential therapy than as the chosen vocation of which she had dreamed.

> They kept my love from me.
>
> In the breaking of sods, there came no hope. With the care of cows was my separation contrived. Alone I continued my way; each day passed as the other, without mercy and without hope. In constant labour I carried my secret and in strange

> fields I laid it low. In the rime of winter and in the drought of summer my love haunted me. His presence pursued me, and the days of remembrance clung like burrs to my side. They would not leave me, nor could I shake them off.[62]

It was only years later, with Reynolds' death, that reconciliation finally came and she reaffirmed the determination to live henceforward in the light of his being. She never saw him again, but he was to remain with her for the rest of her life.

> Though I find him not, he is near me; though I walk not with him, he is beside me. In the vapours of mists he beckons me, and in strange cities he holds my hand.[63]

NOTES

1 Reynolds to Edward Garnett, 17 May 1909, Harold Wright (edited), *Letters of Stephen Reynolds* (London: Hogarth Press, 1923), 123.

2 Philippa Powys diary, 18 and 25 June 1909, in possession of Gerard Casey, Mappowder.

3 Louis Marlow, *Welsh Ambassadors: Powys Lives and Letters* (London: Village Press, 1975), 2.
Kenneth Hopkins in *The Powys Brothers* (Southrepps, Norfolk: Warren House Press, 1972), 147, attributes this quotation to Llewelyn.
For the best brief biography of Katie, see Alyse Gregory, 'Notes on CEPP' (*Powys Review* 20, 1987) 66.

4 Philippa Powys diary, 20–29 February 1908.

5 *Ibid.*, 5 July 1909.

6 Philippa Powys, 'Phoenix *or* Driven Passion', third version, unpublished typescript, University of Texas, 8. This version was probably completed in 1927 or 1928, since the second is dated 1927. A fragment was published in *The Dial*, New York, LXXXV No.2, August 1928.

7 Philippa Powys diary, 5 July 1909.

8 'Phoenix' *op.cit.*, 12.

9 Philippa Powys diary, 5 July 1909.

10 *Ibid.*, 9 July 1909.

11 'Phoenix' *op.cit.*, 12a and 14b.

12 Philippa Powys diary, 9 July 1909.

13 Reynolds to Edward Garnett, 18 June 1909, Texas. Reynolds to John Lane, 15 July 1909, Texas.

14 Philippa Powys diary, 10 July 1909.

15 *Ibid.*, 13–17 July 1909.

16 *Ibid.*, 3 June 1910.

17 *Ibid.*

18 *Ibid.*

19 *Ibid.*

20 *Ibid.*, July 1911.

21 *Ibid.*, 24 February 1910.

22 *Ibid.*, 3 March 1910.

23 Reynolds to Philippa Powys, 7 May 1911, Texas.

24 Philippa Powys diary, August 1911.

25 'Phoenix' *op.cit.*, 15.

26 *Ibid.*, 16.

27 Philippa Powys diary, August 1911.

28 'Phoenix' *op.cit.*, 16.

29 *Ibid.*,17.
30 Philippa Powys diary, August 1911.
31 'Phoenix' *op.cit.*, 18.
32 Philippa Powys diary, August 1911.
33 Reynolds to Philippa Powys, 29 August 1911, Texas.
34 *Ibid.*
35 Philippa Powys diary, October 1911.
36 Reynolds to Philippa Powys, 1 November 1911, Texas.
37 Philippa Powys diary, November 1911.
38 Reynolds to Philippa Powys, 13 March 1912, Texas.
39 'Phoenix' *op.cit.*, 24.
40 Philippa Powys diary, January 1912.
41 In her diary, she refers to Gertrude's presence. In 'Phoenix' *op.cit.*, 31, she talks of walking the sea wall with her brother, most probably Llewelyn who was staying at Montacute at the time.
42 Philippa Powys diary, [August 1912].
43 'Phoenix' *op.cit.*, 24.
44 *Ibid.*, 25.
45 *Ibid.* Judith Stinton in *Chaldon Herring: The Powys Circle in a Dorset Village* (Woodbridge, Suffolk: The Boydell Press, 1988),124, gives the perhaps unintended impression that Reynolds' declaration 'No friends but these, I have' took place when rowing Katie out in his boat, the episode of the previous year. From Ms Stinton's notes, which she very kindly showed me, it is clear that this is not the case.
46 *Ibid.*, 27.
47 *Ibid.*, 28.
48 *Ibid.*, 31.
49 *Ibid.*, 32a.
50 John Cowper Powys to Frances Gregg, 24 August 1912, Oliver Wilkinson (edited), *The Letters of John Cowper Powys to Frances Gregg* (London: Cecil Woolf,1994), 30.
51 John Cowper Powys to Frances Gregg, 22 August 1912, Oliver Wilkinson *op.cit.*, 29.
52 John Cowper Powys to Frances Gregg, 24 August 1912, Oliver Wilkinson *op.cit.*, 30.
53 John Cowper Powys to Frances Gregg, [27 August 1912], Oliver Wilkinson *op.cit.*, 32.
54 John Cowper Powys to Frances Gregg, 25 August 1912, Oliver Wilkinson *op.cit.*, 32.
55 'Phoenix' *op.cit.*, 32a.
56 She wrote a note on 25 August: 'By willing we can walk upon the sea. I have broken the cross Christ is freed and returned to the deserts a child. The moon and the owls are our sisters. The seagulls and ravens help us. Fear thou not much but hope thou not at all. Nietzsche's madness has not been in vain — love from Katie (S.R.)' (John Cowper Powys to Frances Gregg, 25 August 1912, Oliver Wilkinson *op.cit.*, 31).
57 John Cowper Powys to Frances Gregg, [27 August 1912], Oliver Wilkinson *op.cit.*, 33.
58 Reynolds to Philippa Powys, 1 September 1912, in possession of Gerard Casey, Mappowder.
59 'Phoenix' *op.cit.*, 32B.
60 *Ibid.*, 33.
61 *Ibid.*, 37.
62 *Ibid.*, 40.
63 *Ibid.*, 47.

Amorous Life: John Cowper Powys and the Manifestation of Affectivity
H. W. FAWKNER
Crescent Moon Publishing, 1998. Paperback, £7.49 (£6 to Powys Society members). 77pp. ISBN 1 86171 045 3

Rethinking Powys: Critical Essays on John Cowper Powys
Edited by JEREMY ROBINSON
Crescent Moon Publishing, 1999. Paperback, £7.49 (£6 to Powys Society members). 62pp. ISBN 1 86171 046 1

In *Amorous Life* Harold Fawkner is concerned from the first to explore what he perceives to be the universality of John Cowper Powys's achievement. He begins his essay on *Owen Glendower* by establishing a distinction between the novel as a literary entity, and its likely consequences. This sense of dichotomy between the 'work' and its impact lies at the heart of Fawkner's criticism:

> Although the work terminates in the familiar Cowperist conception of enduring, the total impact is such that the idea of the possibility of enduring is shattered. (5)

The second of the two essays which make up this book is on *Weymouth Sands*. Here, he argues, more than in any of Powys's other novels, the author achieves a unity of purpose between the novel and its ultimate effect:

> Here that which is most aesthetic is by the same token that which is most Powysian, most eccentric. For some strange reason, the eccentricity of *Weymouth Sands* is compatible with the principles of traditional aesthetic form — something

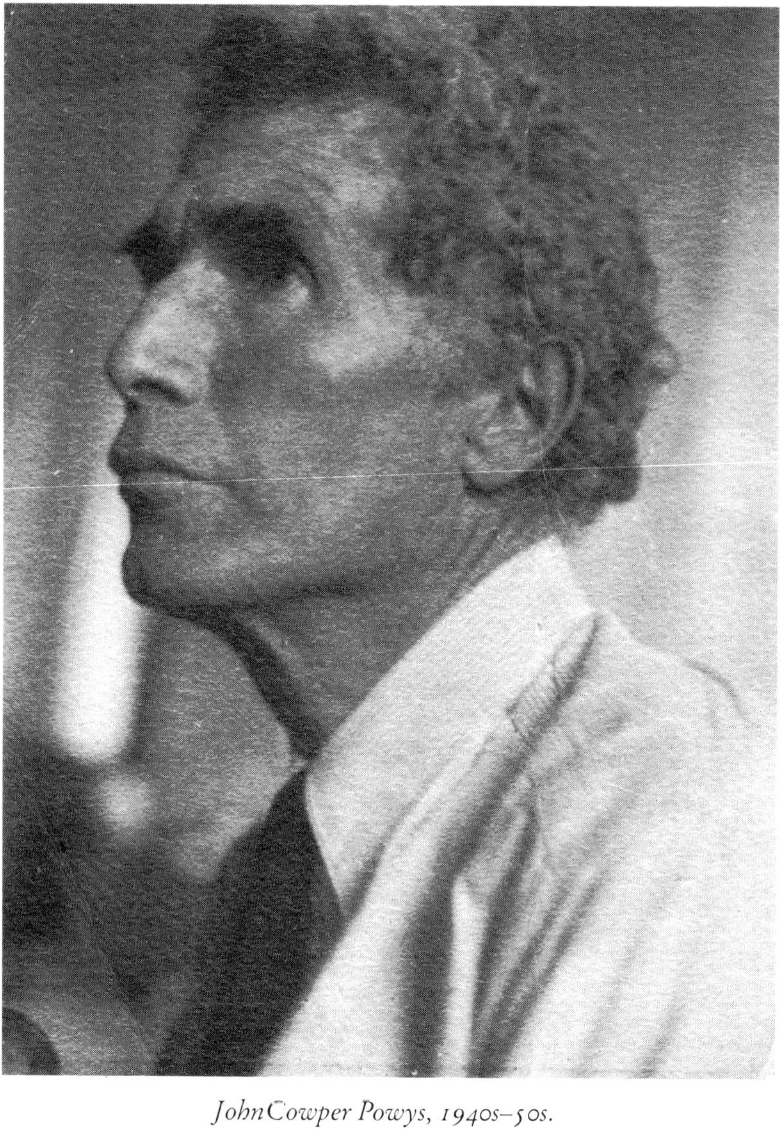

John Cowper Powys, 1940s–50s.

> which we can say of few other works from the hand of this artist. (34)

A fundamental difference between the two novels is of course that *Owen Glendower* is inevitably to be categorised as an historical novel; this will create its own particular tensions. It is an issue that Fawkner explores in some detail in relation to his main theme:

> The decline of chivalry, the destabilization of feudalism, and the installation of the anti-Pope cannot explain the *experience* of historical events any more than 'the breaking down of faith' (624) can explain the merciless, soulless tortures monitored by 'scientists' like Gilles de Pirogue. (6)

History can only explain so much, the subject of 'experience' goes beyond history, and Fawkner discusses the attempts Powys makes to cross that boundary by drawing attention to the way in which the issue of pain is central to both novels:

> There *is* hellish cruelty *because* there is hellish cruelty. There *is* hell because there *is* hell. Hell causes itself. This causing-itself of hell, examined intermittently throughout *Owen Glendower*, is foundational. There is no 'truth' about history which is not a foregrounding of this anomaly. Hence history is itself anomalous ... (6)

Weymouth Sands does not have to negotiate history in the same way, but the novel grapples with fundamentally the same issue. The prospect of a resolution is achieved, Fawkner suggests, through Powys's references to the sea:

> That there can be swallowing totality without any restricting sense of exhaustive totalization, that totality and inexhaustibility are not mutually exclusive — this is what the sea makes us feel, makes us know, and makes us *see*. The 'minute particulars' cannot be extracted from the totality — cannot be 'detached' from 'Weymouth', from the co-presence of the sea, from the 'Absolute' ... (43)

Fawkner is describing an engagement with dualism; he returns repeatedly to observe Powys's awareness of a tension between that which is mundane and that which is not. We are shown how in both novels an incident — an historical incident — is presented to us in a way designed to push our perception of its presence, its 'affectivity', across the boundary that we have been taught to respect as dividing 'matter' from 'spirit'. One particularly helpful example that Fawkner gives is the dismissal of Father Pascentius from Glendower's court. This may be expected to excite mundane responses from the author, from the reader, and from Father Pascentius himself: 'compassion ... commiseration ... self-pity'. What we in fact have is '... the manifest phenomenalization of the originary nature of feeling itself. Even the word 'compassion' is perhaps not quite intimate enough to identify the reality of the pure affective field in which the learned man is finally sighted.' (33)

Fawkner's discussion of *Owen Glendower* begins by considering the significance of Powys's treatment of pain, and as indicated above, it is to pain that he repeatedly returns as the issue that most acutely describes the full extent of Powys's achievement. Pain, the presence of which is so insistent, encapsulates the paradox of being and not-being that Fawkner wishes to explore. Powys, he claims, appears to want us to understand that the 'inhumanity' of pain lies not in its power 'to create human suffering' to the extent that we find ourselves entering 'a sub-human world of brutish negativity'; the inhumanity of pain lies rather in the recognition of its 'mystic god-quality triggering the felt notion that it perhaps has nothing to do with humanity whatsoever — that its horror is the horror of the extraneous.' The paradox here is, of course, that this thing which is 'extraneous', that has 'nothing to do with humanity', also has everything to do with humanity: 'Pain is in this way an indwelling extraneousness in mankind.' Confronted with this, we are forced into a 'reassessment of life'; this is what Powys dares to undertake in *Owen Glendower* and in *Weymouth Sands*; here it is the 'unthinkability of pain' that is explored, whereas in *Wolf Solent*, for example, the issue is side-stepped by a process of objectification (pain is located in the face of the man on the Waterloo steps) (5).

What Fawkner does not do, although in an argument of this kind there is a real danger of this, is to deny the reality of pain. This is not a semantic game designed to neutralise suffering; it is, with Powys, an invitation to think about it differently. In *Weymouth Sands*, he suggests, we understand suffering to be 'a rendezvous with the really intrinsic — with affectivity'. There is a sense in which pain and suffering are describing that meeting point of history and non-history, of the mundane and the numinous, of the intelligible and the unintelligible that takes us beyond the novel as literary entity and into the realm of the writer's full achievement in conjunction with a readership. So this is not therefore to witness a process by which phenomena (of whatever sort) are cancelled out; it is, Fawkner suggests, a 'null-point', a null-point for affectivity; but what that means has to be carefully explained:

> As affectivity, such a null-point is in essence Christian rather than Buddhistic, for the null-point is *felt*, not simply acknowledged as nullity. In no way whatever does 'Weymouth' forward the overall sensation that life is nothingness. Quite the contrary, life is affectivity. (58)

The 'null-point' is 'the immanency of feeling as such' (58).

In the course of these two essays, Fawkner refers to a number of other examples of literary and visual art by way of establishing a context for his discussion. There is no opportunity here to do that aspect of his work justice. His criticism is powerful and complex, and his arguments are compelling.

Fawkner is also represented in *Rethinking Powys*, a collection of four essays edited by Jeremy Robinson. Janina Nordius's '*Wolf Solent* Towards a Discourse of Solitude' is based on part of her full length study of Powys, *'I Am Myself Alone': Solitude and Transcendence in John Cowper Powys* (Göteborg 1997); Ian Hughes's 'The Genre of John Cowper Powys's Major Novels' is a revised version of an article first published in *The Powys Review* in 1986; Joe Boulter's '*The Inmates*, Deleuze/Guattari, Foucault, and Madness' was published in *The Powys Journal*, 1997. Harold Fawkner's essay is 'Venus: Phenomenology of the Beginning of Movement in *A Glastonbury Romance*'.

Janina Nordius discusses the way Powys explores through the

medium of fiction notions of solitude otherwise discussed in *A Philosophy of Solitude* and *In Defence of Sensuality*:

> The personal philosophy that Powys articulated ... can be summed up like this: rather than trying to escape our 'inherent loneliness' by indulging in ... 'drifting, brainless gregariousness', we ought instead to accept it — 'and not only accept it, but find our unique and singular happiness in it'. (5)

To do this we must experience solitude as a 'spiritual state', a state of contemplation that Powys describes as 'an erotic embrace of the not-self by the self'. This is a transcendental state, Nordius suggests 'free from the theocentric connotations that often go with the word' (5). The aim of Powys's philosophy, we are told, 'is to develop a strategy for producing such moments of transcendental solitude by an act of will' (5).

The exposition is clear and helpful; but I felt it also illustrated why it has been so difficult for Powysians to encourage a revival of interest in Powys's philosophical writings. They have not stood the test of time well, which is not necessarily a criticism of the ideas John Cowper wished to disseminate. The appropriate vehicle for what Powys wished to achieve was undoubtedly the novel, and this becomes clear from Nordius's chapter as she discusses the development of character in *Wolf Solent*, and the way in which that novel is plotted. Here we have the opportunity for irony, for doubt, for creative humour; here also we are shown how *Wolf Solent* is an important prerequisite for a full understanding of the fiction that was to follow. Though this is not a part of what Nordius is saying in this essay, an impression is clearly established by the end of it that the philosophical works give way to the novels as the most appropriate medium by which Powys was to express his ideas.

In his essay on *A Glastonbury Romance* Harold Fawkner begins by challenging our fundamental assumptions about 'the book'. He discusses the nature of reading, questioning the way we assume it will be a chronological, lineal experience; he emphasises our holding of the book at the expense of the seeing of it. He involves us in an expertly sustained guessing game, the purpose of which I took to be his intention to re-enact for the reader of this essay what is enacted throughout *A Glastonbury Romance* itself. We are confronted by a sense of infinite possibilities, of the impossibility of certainties, of a constant process of 'movement' playing over the narrative, even where (perhaps especially where) there appears to be no movement of the kind we would normally be looking for. For this novel '... a 'logical' viewpoint is strictly speaking nonsensical ... The medium 'through' which revelation is revealed happens to be revelation itself — this is the prime mystery of life, indeed of revelation.' (24–5) 'Inertia' he argues, 'is understood as movement' (33), and he illustrates this using Powys's description of Crummie standing before a mirror; she is looking at a picture representing Spring, to which is attached a self-portrait, 'Crummie by Crummie, Aged Six'. The moment, we are told, is full of 'furtive movements' (33) for the characters and for the reader in a space where we would not be expected to pause and reflect. What Fawkner is particularly aware of here is the consequence of re-reading, and how in the process the apparent non-event may become charged with meaning; how we as readers may find ourselves 'physically caught in the artefact's reality.' (36)

Ian Hughes approaches the issue of the form of Powys's fiction from a very different critical perspective. Both the previous essays have confirmed in various ways that we are looking at what Powys himself described as 'philosophical romance' (37). As Hughes suggests, this problem of categorisation has been the source of endless anxiety and uncertainty for reviewers. This essay is a thoughtful, well informed work of literary history, contextualising Powys's influences and outlining his development. The main body of the essay concerns itself with the influence of Walter Pater on Powys's *Wood and Stone*, a discussion well worth a second airing. Powys is described as working from the plot of Pater's *Marius the Epicurean*:

> The Paterian thematic structure of *Wood and Stone* recurs in various ways throughout Powys's novels. So rich and adaptable is the pattern, that in most of the rest of his novels Powys is enabled to focus on different and sometimes alternative — but still closely related — aspects of it. (45)

What Nordius has had to say about the philosophical writings of Powys may be set helpfully alongside Hughes on the Paterian influence, as may Hughes's reference to *Wolf Solent* towards the end of this essay. He also has things to say about *Weymouth Sands*, suggesting that it is 'aesthetically perhaps the most pleasing of Powys's novels', and that it 'can be viewed as a set of lyrical variations on the Paterian theme'; this last point is worth taking back to a reading of Fawkner's *Amorous Life*.

Joe Boulter's thesis is that 'there are close analogies between Powys's ideas and those of Foucault and Deleuze/Guattari'; essentially Powys and the post-moderns are pragmatists, and Boulter is particularly interested to observe the application of a pragmatist position to the subject of madness, but he goes on to suggest that 'the pragmatist model is the best starting point for interpreting Powys's work as a whole.' (49) Unlike the other essayists, Boulter expresses a clearly political element within his agenda: 'In *The Inmates* ... Powys repeatedly makes direct connections between the designation of madness and the preservation of institutions of political power.' (50) It is a compelling argument that establishes Powys's work as profoundly relevant to literary criticism and the world it seeks to reflect in the early twenty-first century. We can recognise without too much difficulty the Powys revealed by Nordius, Fawkner and Hughes in the pragmatist described by Boulter; he is an author determined to reveal and sustain a plurality of worlds. For Powys, Boulter suggests, Freud and Jung each construct no more than 'just another world version, without any particular claim to be true' (54). Against this we have Foucault arguing that madness has 'its own validity'. The Powysian solution, enacted in *The Inmates*, is a retreat from 'oppositionality', in the novel this becomes literally a bid to escape from that which has designated them 'mad'. Boulter, like Fawkner, is making a powerful case for the recognition of John Cowper Powys as a novelist who addresses issues that reside at the heart of our contemporary political, cultural and social environment.

Jeremy Robinson's Introduction to the book is clear and helpful. He considers the history of the critical reception of John Cowper Powys, and he has interesting things to say on characterisation and plot in Powys's novels. He finds it no easier than any of his predecessors to explain with any certainty why Powys has not attracted the following that other writers of his generation have. He also informs us that *Rethinking Powys* is the first in a new series of collections of essay on John Cowper Powys. That is good news.

[Crescent Moon publications can be obtained directly from Crescent Moon Publishing, P. O. Box 393, Maidstone, Kent ME14 5XU, U.K. Telephone 01622 729593; e-mail jrobinson@crescentmoon.org.uk]

A Severe Case of Dandruff

HERBERT WILLIAMS

Gomer Press, 1999. Paperback, £5.95. 152pp. ISBN 1 85902 773 3

It is the late 1940s, Ralph is 16, his brother Bobby has already died of tuberculosis, and now he himself has been diagnosed as having the disease. Rather than refer directly to TB by name, it was customary to call it 'a severe case of dandruff' because it was the 'dandruff' cases that survived. Ralph is sent from his home in Aberystwyth to a sanatorium in the Brecon Beacons.

This is at once a novel that delivers a vivid sense of its post-war historical moment, while at the same time demanding to be read for its relevance to our own late twentieth-, early twenty-first-century condition. In his Introduction, Alun Richards points out that at the time when the novel is set, the terror induced by the letters TB is to be compared with the reaction to AIDS in our own time. It is a rites-of-passage novel, and in this sense there is also a timelessness to the drama of Ralph's coming of age in the intimidating surroundings of the sanatorium and its occupants.

Despite the impression that may have been given so far, the novel is anything but melodramatic. Williams is an accomplished poet, and in this book he shows himself to be a master of understatement, economy, and finely judged rhythmic prose. The anxiety, fear and confusion that Ralph experiences become more palpable because the author is prepared to let the situation speak for itself. The atmosphere is charged with sexual and class tensions among the young inmates, tensions made more oppressive and poignant by the uncertainty of their future. It is a situation realised all the more vividly by the fact that Williams gives us an unvarnished record of the way in which a number of Ralph's fellow patients give vent to their anger and frustration through an adolescent crudity of language, a language of ironic and casual profanity that assumes its own institutional status, though it can still shock.

Ralph's sense of bewilderment and isolation, his passion for a local girl, the identity crisis he experiences when a bereavement means that he returns home for a brief period, achieve the impact they do because Williams scrupulously avoids sensationalist prose. The one moment where he does allow himself a more lurid descriptive voice is where Ralph visits a dying patient; and for this reason he creates one of the most memorable, darkest, and troubling moments in the book.

The subject may not sound a particularly inviting one, yet — as with so many successful rites-of-passage novels — the effect of the whole is without doubt affirmative, and I would expect that readers of this novel will find themselves moved, not infrequently amused, and in the end certainly grateful to Herbert Williams for 'a severe case of dandruff'.

Reliquaries

PATRICIA V. DAWSON

Hub Editions, 1999. Paperback, £4.99. 52pp. ISBN *1 870653 947*

As a title for a collection of poems, *Reliquaries* might well give the impression that the contents were likely to be elegaically sombre. Nothing could be further from the truth in Patricia V. Dawson's latest book. There is some moving, reflective writing, but Dawson also establishes herself as a poet endowed with sharp observational powers, frequently noting seemingly trivial or quirky events from which she creates poetry of wit, often spiced with a delicious seasoning of black comedy. Having a wasps' nest destroyed is 'good advice', but it is also the occasion for sadism:

> 'They'll all go in,' he said,
> 'get poison on them and then die.'
> Standing in my bedroom,

with the window closed,
he put his hand
flat against the glass.
The wasps, a crowd of them,
realised something was wrong,
rushed at his palm,
attacking madly and he laughed,
taunting them. He did it once again.

There remains, not surprisingly, a lingering sense of unease about what was supposed to be the final solution:

Five weeks have gone.
Although the nest is out of action,
wasps have come,
flying to and fro in the vicinity.
Every time I climb up
on the roof or loiter
in the garden,
one comes and bothers me,
Wasps are cute.
Take my advice
and never cross a wasp.
('Wasps')

She can also turn doggerel to thought-provoking use:

Our lives are made up of decisions —
whether we will or we won't.
And now we are asked
to decide at the last
whether we do or we don't.

The pundits are prone to debate it,
whether we can or we can't
deprive God of the power
to decide any hour
whether we are or we aren't.
('Euthanasia')

Dawson observes events and people with equal objectivity; her topics range from all kinds of art, including jazz, to old age, to mature students, and from genetic engineering to the press in a variety of guises:

> The Press, not easy to define,
> behaves in manner serpentine,
> a beast that preys upon the herd
> yet feeds it with the printed word.
> A looking-glass in which it sees
> the evidence of its disease?
> Such candour we could never buy,
> for don't we all prefer a lie
> that boosts our ego and portrays
> our sins as sweet and winning ways?
> ('A Strange Animal')

The death of Princess Diana occasions a number of sideways looks in the course of the book, including reflections on Harrods and its owner:

> Bless you, Mr Fayed.
> You're every bit as great
> as that dear old Mr Fezziwig
> you try to imitate.
> ('The Knightsbridge Charity Rag')

A specific interrogation of the properties of words themselves and the process of naming informs the meaning of all these poems. In the case of 'Gender Bending' this is combined with the importance of a sense of place, another theme that recurs throughout the volume:

> When I was a child,
> cars were feminine,
> sharing the humanity of ships.
> Now, more common,
> they are its.
> But on the borders of Wales,
> where there is no neuter,

gadgets are sexed.
Freezers, for instance,
are males.
Are such definitions easily arrived at,
or are they disputed
in bars and markets
where farmers, who
castrate their beasts,
pronounce the curse of Adam
on machines?

Even in the more serious, reflective poems, an impish sense of humour is rarely far away. In the case of the final, fine poem, 'The Baharcus Tree', we are given a word of uncertain origin. 'Baharcus': was it a made-up name, like 'snimny', part of a private 'pet vocabulary', or is it a real word? The answer is that, regardless of its origins, it is indeed a 'real' word, the meaning of which goes far beyond the tree it labels, the tree that is to be found at the place where the couple would go:

... to see a Tuscan view that stretched below
the east side of the Malverns
at their southern tip.

Here as elsewhere there is a constant passage in and out of a series of realities, of interleaved truths (the Tuscan view, the Malverns, the tree, the tree's name). With the perception of an artist who is a sculptor, printmaker, who produces paintings, drawings and etchings besides poetry, Dawson explores her subject with a knowledge of its infinite possibilities:

I can't remember whether this
was one of the imaginary names
that he'd invented when he was a child.
His pet vocabulary was full of them.
Snimny, for instance, for that indeterminate stuff
like thistledown, but not; like woodash,
but not quite. It suddenly appears and floats.
It falls like snow, or household fluff shaken

from a duster. We never quite knew what it was,
but when we saw it, hailed it.

The final stanza of 'The Baharcus Tree' focuses with a wonderful economy on the inadequacy of the mundane, on the superiority of the eccentric, the individually, spontaneously realised meaning as against the quotidian word, the would-be authority of the official pronouncement:

I've tried to buy a rosebush
to remember him, but know
that he would not have noticed it
the way he noticed the Baharcus tree
that grows beside the road,
without a proper name, outside the churchyard,
but more permanent than news or snimny.

The first poem in the volume is a haiku, inspired by a fourteenth-century reliquary said to contain the hand of St Patrick:

Gloved in silver,
the bones of
a saint's hand.

There are a number of haiku, haiku sequences, and poems that make use of the haiku style throughout the book. Dawson builds her extended pieces on haiku foundations with considerable success; two particularly interesting examples are 'The Farmer at St Benoit' and 'Mended China Animals'. Again, it becomes clear that the poet's experience of working in the media of visual and sculpted art is an important influence on the literary achievement. 'The Farmer at St Benoit' is a poem that contains a series of vividly realised vignettes that we might be looking at as we wander through a gallery:

When his cream car
arrives, his Charolais appear
on the horizon.

'A Journey to the Hiroshige Exhibition at the Sachler Gallery' is one of several poems where the link with sculpted and visual art is made explicit.

In the end, I think it is the range and variety exhibited by the 49 poems in this book which makes it such an impressive volume. The reader can never assume they know what is coming next, and from reading to reading of individual poems the emphasis will constantly be shifting, what initially registered as a light-hearted piece can return as something far more disturbing. We are invited here to reflect on the fragile continuities of our lives, continuities constructed from words, visual images, from memories; we find ourselves looking askance at the present, which only ever pretends to be knowable, waiting for the next move, watching 'the woman in the passage almost turning':

In the doctor's waiting room
I find a picture
that I know so well.
As a child I used to lie
and look at it
on the bedroom wall.
— A mother at her doorway
with a little girl.
Their clothes are cumbersome and long.
There is a woman
walking down a passage,
her back to me.
She almost turns.
I think I see
her red skirt move.

My mother slept.
I dared not wake her.
Birds were singing in the garden.
All my plans were stalled.
The day began without me.
Now, at seventy, I wait again
watching the picture people,
the woman in the passage almost turning.
('De Hooch at the Surgery')

John Williams

NOTES ON CONTRIBUTORS

GLEN CAVALIERO is the President of The Powys Society. He is a member of the English Faculty of Cambridge University. Recent publications include a collection of poems, *Steeple on a Hill* (1997) and *The Alchemy of Laughter: Comedy in English Fiction* (2000).

PETER J. FOSS is a writer and painter. His book on the Battle of Bosworth, *The Field of Redemore*, was republished in 1998 and he has also recently published a book on the diary of Joseph Moxon, 1798–99. He is a former editor of *The Powys Journal* and has published and lectured widely on the works of Llewelyn Powys.

STEPHEN POWYS MARKS is an architect, editor and writer, and is the Honorary Treasurer of The Powys Society. He has contributed extensively to Powys studies, especially in the *Newsletter*, and to other publication work of the Society.

J. LAWRENCE MITCHELL is a Professor and Head of Department of English at Texas A&M University. A specialist in linguistics, he has published widely, and continues to work on a biography of T. F. Powys.

PAUL ROBERTS is currently Chairman of The Powys Society having previously edited the *Newsletter* for ten years. He has published many articles in the field of Powys studies and has edited a number of works by John Cowper Powys.

CHRISTOPHER SCOBLE is a former administrator at the Home Office where, in the late 1980s, he was head of the Broadcasting Department. He is currently working on a new edition of Stephen Reynolds' *A Poor Man's House*.

JOHN WILLIAMS is Reader in Literary Studies at the University of Greenwich. He has published a number of articles on T. F. Powys; his most recent book is *Mary Shelley: A Literary Life*, published in March 2000. He edited *The Powys Journal* from 1997 to 1999.

ADVISORY BOARD

THE POWYS JOURNAL: INDEX TO VOLUMES I TO X

Editors

Peter J. Foss (Vols I–III, VI, *Joint Editor* for Vols IV & V),
Louise de Bruin (*Deputy Editor* for Vols I–III, *Joint Editor* for Vols IV & V),
J. R. Williams (Vols VII–IX), Paul Roberts (Vol. X)
and Charles Lock (*Contributing Editor*, Vols I–X)

References to all articles and contributors, every review, and every illustration, are included in this compilation. The first four sections of the Index constitute the SUBJECT INDEX. It is divided so that everything connected with each of the three principal writers can be found under his own heading; this is followed by a General Index which picks up all other references and articles, together with the dates of birth and death of most of the persons listed. Authors of articles and reviews are shown in parentheses, those of reviews being preceded by 'review,'. CONTRIBUTORS are listed in the last section. Articles marked with an asterisk were originally given as papers at meetings of the Society, some having been substantially revised for publication.

In the first three sections, material has been divided into the following categories:

A. the author's own writing reproduced in the *Journal*, in date order as far as can be ascertained, with related material;
B. commentary and other references relating to single published works, in order of first publication;
C. other commentary and references;
D. portraits: photographs first, then drawings.

The following initials have been used where appropriate for members of the Montacute family of Powys:

ARP	Albert Reginald	GMP	Gertrude Mary	JCP	John Cowper
CEPP	Catharine Edith Philippa	LAP	Lucy Amelia	MCP	Mary Cowper
CFP	Charles Francis	LCP	Littleton Charles	TFP	Theodore Francis
EMP	Emily Marian	LP	Llewelyn	WEP	William Ernest

Stephen Powys Marks

JOHN COWPER POWYS

A.

B.

C.

D.

T. F. POWYS

A.

B.

C.

D.

LLEWELYN POWYS

A.

B.

C.

D.

GENERAL INDEX

CONTRIBUTORS